The Egyptian Gods and Goddesses

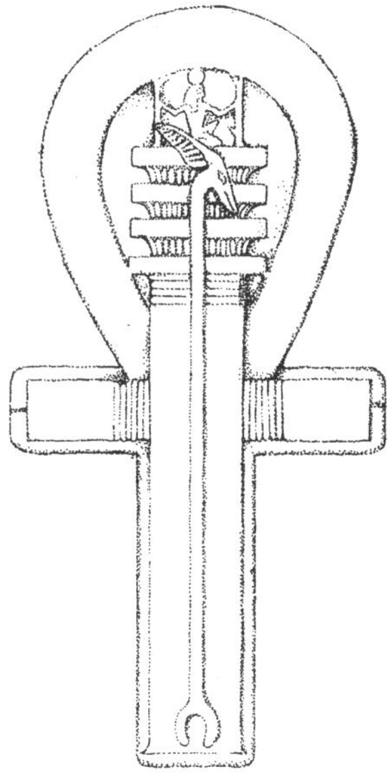

The Egyptian Gods and Goddesses

The Mythology and Beliefs of Ancient Egypt

Clive Barrett

DIAMOND
BOOKS

To Monty
In memory of Montgomery Jones
a cat of great character

This edition published 1996 by
Diamond Books
77-85 Fulham Palace Road
Hammersmith, London W6 8JB

First published in the UK by the Aquarian Press 1992

ISBN 0 261 66930 3

Printed and bound in Great Britain by
Creative Print and Design (Wales), Ebbw Vale

Contents

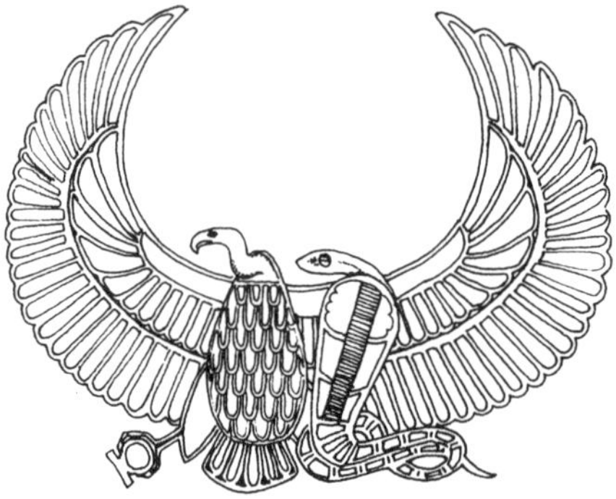

Introduction

The 'gift of the Nile' was how the ancient Greek historian Herodotus described the land of the Egyptians.

Without the Nile there would be no Egypt. Its annual flooding gave life to the long valley through which it passed, it watered the crops and enriched the soil, providing life in the midst of the desert.

The Egyptians were acutely aware of this dependence, that their very existence was subject to the whim of the river. In the inundation the Nile brought rich black mud from its many tributaries and deposited it along its course. The Egyptians named their land 'Kem', 'the black land', and strove ceaselessly to extract every last part to make the most of their annual gift. They constructed banks to prevent over-flooding and dug irrigation channels to guide the precious liquid to the once barren land.

Beyond the cultivated fields lay the dessert: 'Dvrt', 'the red land'. This contrast between the fertile and the barren was so deeply impressed upon the Egyptians that the colours black and red became synonymous with good and evil respectively.

The main occupation of the people was agriculture. The cultivated land was rich and its produce abundant, animals were domesticated and fish and foul caught. But if the annual flood failed to appear, the Nile would become low, the crops would fail and the people starved.

The Nile also provided flax and papyrus for the manufacture of clothing and writing paper. The surrounding hills gave stone of various grades of hardness and workability which was used for both building and decorative carving. Wood, however, had to be imported—cedar coming from Lebanon and Syria, as few trees grew in the Nile valley.

Beneath the burning sun, between the inhospitable deserts, the Egyptian clung to the Nile for life.

History of Egypt

Paleolithic Period—the Old Stone Age

There are traces of man living in the Nile valley before 12,000 BCE. These were nomadic hunters and gatherers who manufactured tools of stone, often producing well-fashioned items and displaying great skill. We know that they hunted wild cattle, antelope and, on rarer occasions, wild ass and hippopotamus. They were excellent fishermen and ate a variety of shellfish. Bird bones have also been discovered in great quantities, revealing that they were skilled in snaring and netting.

There is evidence (from plant silica found on the stone implements) to suggest that plants were cultivated to some degree at this time. However for a long period the Nile valley was subject to a series of high floods which curtailed any advances that may have been made in the field of agriculture, and once again man turned to hunting, with a special emphasis on fishing. This way of life remained virtually unchanged until about 5200 BCE, when a new people from the west began to enter the Nile valley and settled around the oasis of Faiyum. These people were farmers, and kept cattle, sheep, pigs and goats. They also cultivated crops of wheat, barley and flax.

Then followed a period of about a thousand years during which the native population learned the skills of agriculture from the newcomers and left their hunting life to become farmers. Beginning in the north in the region of the Delta, the change spread south into Upper Egypt. This appears to have happened peacefully as no signs of aggression have been discovered between the new and the old peoples.

By Neolithic times (the New or Late Stone Age), man had begun to live in fixed settlements and had gained agricultural skills. This change from a nomadic to a settled life, from a mainly hunting life to a farming one, occurred somewhat later in Egypt than elsewhere. However by about 4000 BCE, the Egyptians were building permanent dwellings and making pottery vessels.

Even at this early date a strong belief in the afterlife is evident, for bodies have been found buried with food, tools and other items essential for life in the next world. The inclusion of finely made stone pallets for grinding cosmetics reveals a highly developed state of sophistication.

Finally there emerged a civilization that was to remain virtually unchanged for the next 4,000 years. The Egyptians were a conservative people and their culture was to remain intact, despite contact with outsiders, occasional waves of immigration by new settlers and even invasions and conquests.

Throughout this period the thin strip of habitable land that snaked through the desert to the sea was divided into a series of tribal lands known as 'Nomes'. Each Nome consisted of a number of villages or towns lying upon the banks of the Nile, which provided them with water for their crops and animals and also a means of transport. The Nomes, of which there were 20 in Lower Egypt and 22 in Upper Egypt, were governed by chieftains who usually lived close to the temple of the tribal god or goddess, thus combining from an early date the links between secular and spiritual authority.

Around the beginning of the fourth millennium BCE the various tribal Nomes began to group together, forming larger and stronger political units. Eventually the whole of Upper Egypt fell under the control of a single leader. This gave the southern confederacy the power and strength to bring its influence to bear on the still largely unorganized Nomes of Lower Egypt, thus moving for the first time towards a single country. The process of unification was finally completed around the year 3500 BCE by King Menes, the first king of both northern and southern Egypt and founder of the First Dynasty. He based his capital at Memphis.

The Old Kingdom

The First Dynasty was a time of great change. With the new stability of strong political control, the arts developed and architecture produced massive building

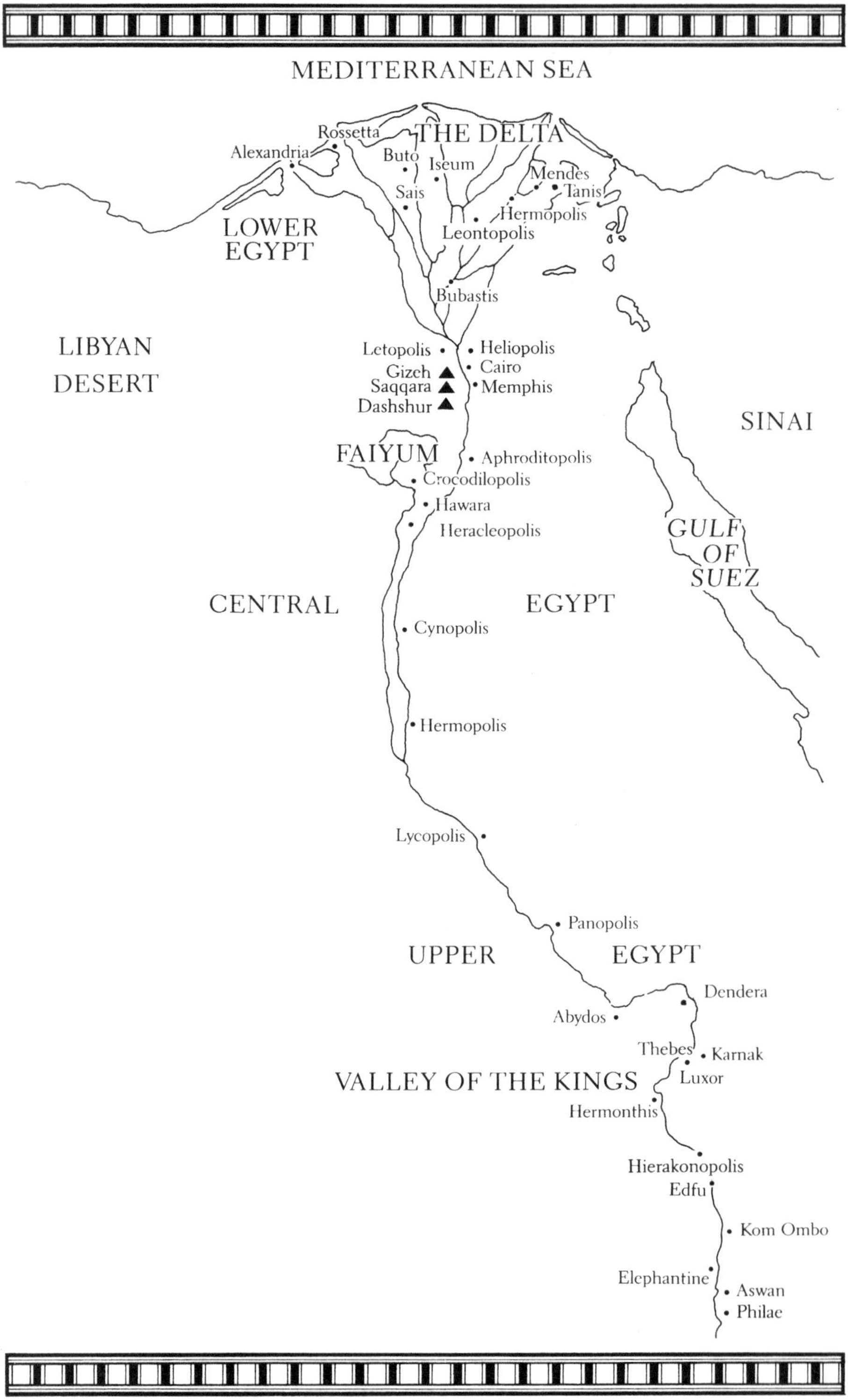
MEDITERRANEAN SEA
Rossetta
THE DELTA
Alexandria
Buto
Iseum
Mendes
Tanis
Sais
Hermopolis
Leontopolis
LOWER EGYPT
Bubastis
LIBYAN DESERT
Letopolis
Heliopolis
Gizeh
Cairo
Saqqara
Memphis
Dashshur
SINAI
FAIYUM
Aphroditopolis
Crocodilopolis
Hawara
Heracleopolis
GULF OF SUEZ
CENTRAL EGYPT
Cynopolis
Hermopolis
Lycopolis
Panopolis
UPPER EGYPT
Dendera
Abydos
Thebes
Karnak
VALLEY OF THE KINGS
Luxor
Hermonthis
Hierakonopolis
Edfu
Kom Ombo
Elephantine
Aswan
Philae

Key

NOMES OF LOWER EGYPT

A White Wall
B Foreleg
C West
D Southern Shield
E Northern Shield
F Mountain Bull
G Western Harpoon
H Eastern Harpoon
I Andjety
J Black Ox
K Ox-count
L Calf and Cow
M Prospering Sceptre
N Foremost of the East
O Ibis
P Fish
Q Behdit
R Prince of the South
S Prince of the North
T Plumed Falcon of Sopedu

THE NOMES OF UPPER EGYPT

1 Ta-Sety
2 Throne of Horus
3 Shrine
4 Sceptre
5 Two Falcons
6 Crocodile
7 Sistrum
8 Great Land
9 Min
10 Cobra
11 Seth
12 Viper Mount
13 Upper Sycamore and Viper
14 Lower Sycamore and Viper
15 Hare
16 Oryx
17 Jackal
18 Anti
19 Two Sceptres
20 Southern Sycamore
21 Northern Sycamore
22 Knife

works, the like of which had never been seen before. The lands of the Nubian tribes were conquered, and military expeditions reached even further south. Papyrus paper was manufactured for the first time and by the end of the First Dynasty hieroglyphic writing was being developed. Craftsmen were experimenting with intricate forms of jewellery, and furniture too became much more complex and refined.

During the Second Dynasty these changes were taken further, but the Nile's strength began to combat the advances of man. For a period of some 200 years the rainfall in eastern Africa was reduced by one third, causing the annual floods to drop by between one and one-and-a-half metres. This had a direct and drastic effect on the agriculture and the ability of the land to support its growing population. Famine and plagues became the norm for years on end, which resulted in political unrest and instability. Taking advantage of Egypt's difficulties, the desert tribes attacked over the ill-defended borders, and about 2700 BCE there was an armed rebellion which almost toppled the Dynasty and come close to reducing the country to chaos.

The rulers of the Third Dynasty, however, appear to have overcome their problems, helped by a return to stable weather conditions and a reliable and predictable Nile. It was during this period of the Old Kingdom that the state became all-powerful, with the king being regarded as divine, although it was not until the Fifth Dynasty that he was considered to be the equal of the gods. Under the guidance of the divine kings the irrigation system was expanded and improved. In the Third Dynasty the royal architect Imhotep designed and built for his master what was then the largest stone structure built by man—the step pyramid at Saqqara. The buildings and courtyards surrounding the pyramid were enclosed within a wall of over a mile in length.

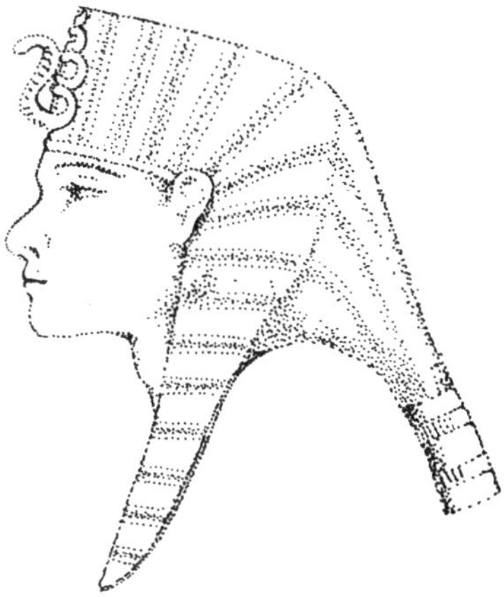

It was in the Fourth Dynasty that the true pyramid appeared, and those of Cheops, Chephren and Mycennus at Gizeh represent the high point of the art of pyramid building. But by the Fifth Dynasty the Egyptians' ability had so declined that today we find that the later pyramids are little more than shapeless mounds of rubble.

Kings were laid to rest in the pyramids themselves, while around the pyramid base the tombs of government officials were constructed. High positions within Egyptian society were reserved for the king's relatives, often the sons of his minor queens. These people would serve him faithfully during life in the firm belief that they might share his divine immortality by serving him after death in the other world. At this time it was believed that only the king was immortal by birth—to others immortality was only obtainable if the king consented to the individual being buried in close proximity to the royal grave. Those who were especially favoured were granted permission to build their tombs in the shadow of the pyramid itself.

The time for building and the necessary manpower were found in the period of the annual inundation of the Nile. When the flood waters washed over the cultivated land the peasant was unable to continue his agricultural work, so he would be employed on one of the great state construction projects. This involved building temples, digging canals for irrigation, working in quarries cutting stone or whatever else might be required.

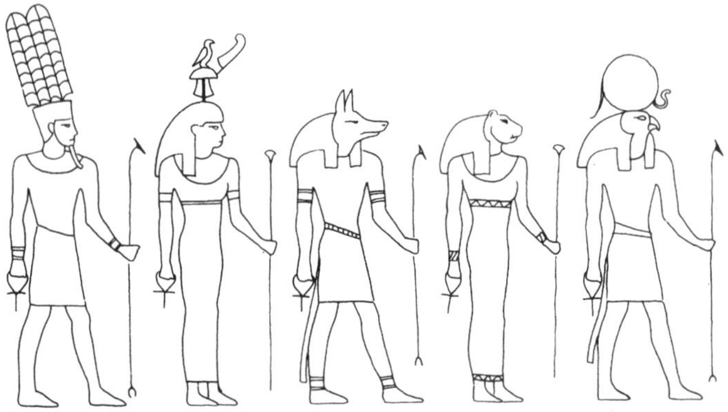

Amun-Ra Amunet Anubis Bast Harakhte

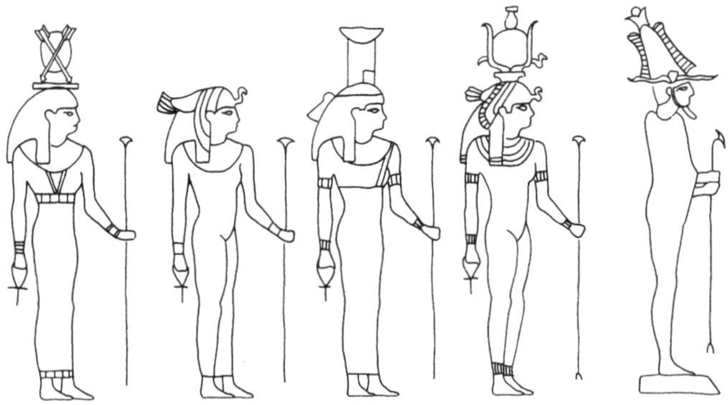

Neit Nekhebet Nephthys Nut Osiris

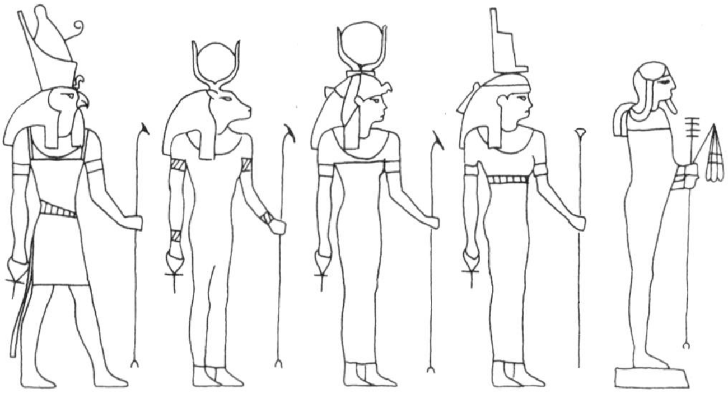

Horus Hathor Isis Isis Khonsu

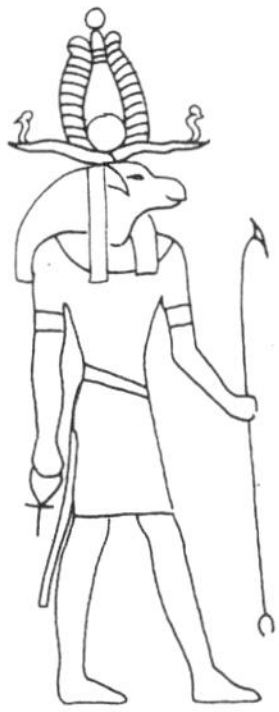
Khnum

Ma'at

Mut

Min

Neit

Osiris

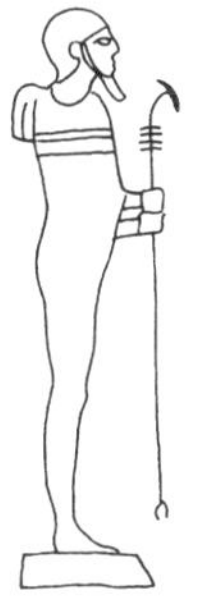
Ptah

Sebek

Set

Sekhmet

Shu

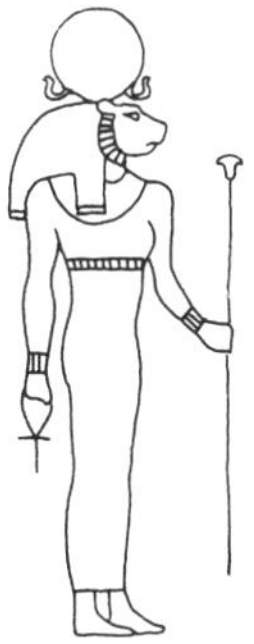
Tefnut

Thoth

Neferten

Hapi

The king was believed to govern the sun, the earth and the Nile. Without his aid the people would not survive, so they worked diligently to ensure his survival after death. Thus the hard work of the peasants supported the king both in life and after death.

As the art of pyramid building reached its zenith in the Fourth Dynasty, so did the creative arts in other fields, including sculpture, jewellery-making and painting, but following this came a gradual slide into material poverty, which finally tumbled into anarchy, pushed by a combination of social, economic and religious factors. Although Egyptian civilization rose again in the Fifth Dynasty, its subsequent achievement never surpassed nor even equalled that of the Fourth Dynasty.

With the Fifth Dynasty came the rise to power of the sun god Ra. His main cult centre was Heliopolis, the city of the sun. As the god's popularity increased so did the influence of his priests. This was eventually to the detriment of the king, who now became known as the son of Ra, thus moving into second place behind the high priest of Heliopolis. The kings of this period also began to marry outside their immediate family, which had the effect of diminishing their claim to divinity.

The cost of maintaining the royal palaces was enormous, and brought problems to the pharaoh. Royal expenditure began to outstrip its income, which was derived mainly from the land. There had been a tradition of presenting nobles with gifts of land, the income of which paid for the upkeep of their own tombs. This land, together with that of the temples (also gifts of the king), was often exempt from taxation. So eventually a large proportion

of the land in Egypt was generating no income for the royal treasury.

As land passed from father to son, the land lords became further and further removed from the royal family and consequently their dependence and allegiance declined. They began to set themselves up as independent kings. Artists and craftsmen gathered around them, their services no longer being affordable by the increasingly impoverished pharaoh, and they began to build and decorate elaborate tombs for their new patrons.

First Intermediate Period

With the end of the Sixth Dynasty, Egypt entered into a period of rapid decline. Against a background of anarchy and

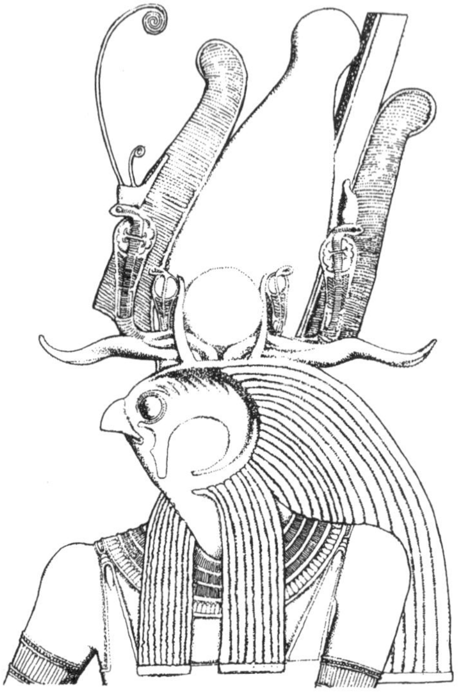

violence the kings vainly attempted to retain central control from their capital at Memphis. It was a time of uncertainty and instability. According to Manetho, the Greek historian, 70 kings ruled for 70 days, but this may refer to a collection of nobles trying to hold the country together rather than a quick succession of rulers.

Internal chaos continued into throughout the Seventh and into the Eighth Dynasty. The problems of the rulers were made worse by a series of crop failures, and famine was followed by plague. Marauding bands of thieves roamed the land at will, taking advantage of the lack of effective governmental control, while from outside Egypt came the nomadic tribes of the desert, penetrating far into the Delta. Egypt was reduced to the situation that had existed prior to unification centuries before, with the local Nomarchs becoming independent rulers, each attempting to restore order in their own locality.

Then Achthoes of the Twentieth Nome assumed the name Meryibre and became the king of an area of Middle Egypt, thus founding the Ninth Dynasty. Ruling from Heracleopolis, he slowly restored stability to his kingdom. From Meryibre the kings of the Ninth and Tenth Dynasties were descended.

This period of unrest had, however, altered the Egyptians' outlook on life profoundly. The local governors considered themselves to be of equal standing to the king, and so claimed the right to a continued life after death. This idea spread to the ordinary members of society, until the whole population felt that it could look forward to a continued existence in the afterlife. As a direct consequence of this change in attitude towards death, worship of the god Osiris, once the sole preserve of the king, became popular amongst all classes. This also had the effect of decentralizing belief. Not until Osiris became the head of the state religion did the king regain his influence on the spiritual thoughts of the populace.

The Middle Kingdom

About the year 2040 BCE Menthotep I of Thebes organized the independent Nomes to fight against the kings of Heracleopolis. Eventually his son Mentuhotep II defeated the ruler of the Middle Kingdom and reunited the whole of Egypt. He founded the Eleventh Dynasty and during his 51 years as king restored Egypt to her former prosperity, securing her borders and protecting trade routes. After a break of many years cedar wood was again imported from Lebanon. His son Mentuhotep III followed with a peaceful reign, but with Mentuhotep IV unrest returned in the form of a southern governor named Amenemmes.

Overthrowing the Theban king, Amenemmes took the throne and founded the Twelfth Dynasty. He moved his capital from Thebes to the more centrally positioned Itlowe, near the Faiyum, an oasis in a natural basin. He re-established pyramid building (examples of Middle Kingdom pyramids may be found at Lisht, Dahshur El-Lahun and Hawara), and once again *mastaba* tombs were constructed in the shadow of the pyramids for high-ranking court officials.

At this time a return was made to highly organized administration, enabling complex irrigation work to be executed, and a vast engineering project was begun at the Faiyum. The annual inflow of water from the Nile was reduced, thus limiting local flooding, and further flood defences were constructed, along with numerous dykes and canals. The final result was that the lake became a well-managed reservoir and over 40 square miles of new pasture land was reclaimed.

At the beginning of the Middle Kingdom full privileges and powers had been restored to the Nomarchs, but they soon began to abuse them, leaving the king with no alternative but to suppress their activities. From that time onwards the Nomes were no longer alternative political centres: control over taxation, troop raising and the law courts was removed to the capital.

Following the demise of the Nomarchs a new middle class emerged, consisting of artisans, small farmers and traders. All were

duly grateful and loyal to the king for their new-found status.

Egypt, now in a position to expand its borders, looked towards Nubia. A military force was dispatched to secure its conquest, following which a string of powerful fortresses was constructed to consolidate the new possession.

From Nubia came gold, although the Egyptians still had to import much-needed copper and granite. Remains have been discovered indicating that during this period there was an Egyptian presence in Palestine, Syria and Sinai. In these places the presence of the Egyptian army ensured untroubled trading and mining. Trade also prospered in the Mediterranean and the Aegean. Copper and bronze are known to have been imported from Cyprus.

The skills of the Egyptian craftsmen producing fine jewellery reached new heights during this period. Their work using lapis lazuli, amethyst and carnelian set in gold was never surpassed. It was also the Egyptians' golden age of literature, works dating from this time being held above all others for their refinement.

The Twelfth Dynasty eventually came to a close, however, with Queen Sobeknefew, who failed to provide an heir to the throne, thus leaving the succession uncertain.

The Second Intermediate Period

The precise sequence of Dynasties during the Second Intermediate Period has not been established. It would appear, however, that the Twelfth and Thirteenth Dynasties ran concurrently, with their kings ruling different parts of Egypt and two centres of control at Memphis and Xois. Of the Fourteenth Dynasty little is known.

Asiatic settlers, known as Hyksos people, who had entered Egypt in the Middle Kingdom, now saw a chance to assume control of the country. Their leader Salitis took Memphis in 1672 BCE and founded the Fifteenth Dynasty. Egypt was to remain under Hyksos rule throughout the Sixteenth Dynasty. The Hyksos kings brought many new ideas to Egypt. They popularized the lyre and the lute, and promoted the use of the vertical loom, but their main interests were of a military nature. They introduced bronze weapons, replacing the inferior copper variety, and also developed the use of the horse and chariot in warfare. From that time onwards Egypt was more aggressive towards its neighbours, keeping a permanent standing army and pursuing a definite policy of empire building.

The end of the Hyksos period began when a Seventeenth Dynasty king, Seqenenre, formerly prince of Thebes, claimed the throne and instigated military action against the Hyksos King Apophis. The mummified remains of King Seqenenre have been discovered, the head of which bears horrific wounds, strongly suggesting that he died in battle. His son Kamose later defeated the Hyksos army and took their capital at Avaris.

The New Kingdom

About 1570 BCE the founder of the Eighteenth Dynasty was Amosis, the son of Kamose. He followed his father's successes against the Hyksos by driving them out of Egypt, then to prevent their return he pursued them far into Palestine. He was a strong king, and conquered many foreign countries.

With the spoils of war and tributes from

the defeated peoples swelling the royal treasury, Egypt became wealthier than ever before. Magnificent temples and tombs were built, Nubia was brought under Egyptian control once more and the fortresses of the Middle Kingdom were repaired and expanded. Many new fortresses were also constructed. Further campaigns of conquest brought the Syrian states and Palestine under Egyptian rule. The sons of the native governors were brought back to Egypt as hostages, and after being subjected to the best of Egyptian education and culture they were returned as loyal subjects of the pharaoh to their homelands.

The kings of this Dynasty had other interests, as may be seen from their tombs in the Valley of the Kings on the west bank of the Nile, the splendour of which was revealed by the discovery of the tomb of Tutankhamun, one of their last kings. King Amenophis constructed a vast mortuary temple which once stood behind the colossi of Memnon, while another king, Tuthmosis, is known to have had a concern for natural history. During his wars in Syria he collected many examples of unusual plants and animals which he dispatched to Egypt to be kept in his palace gardens.

The efforts of a line of strong and active kings made Egypt powerful and prosperous. However this came to an end in 1425 BCE with Amenophis III, who paid little attention to affairs of state. His son Akhenaten, preoccupied with his religious reforms, cared even less. Therefore with the growth of the Assyrian and Hittite powers Egypt's empire began to disintegrate, and by the end of the Eighteenth Dynasty it had all but ceased to exist.

Following the death of Tutankhamun, Akhenaten's son and successor, a non-royal advisor named Ay assumed the throne. He married the royal widow to legitimatize his rule, but she wrote to the king of the Hittites asking him to send one of his sons to take the throne as her husband. However the Hittite king delayed and when eventually a prince was dispatched he was intercepted and killed by the followers of Ay.

Ay was succeeded by Horemheb, who spent most of his reign restoring the cult of Amun, which Akhenaten had suppressed.

The founder of the Nineteenth Dynasty was Ramesses, the vizier of Horemheb. Under his son Sethos I, the priesthood of Amun regained their former power. The capital of Egypt was transferred to Pi Ramesse, also known as Avaris. New temples were built and the empire was retaken. Ramesses II, who succeeded his father Sethos I, conquered much of Asia Minor, including Syria, and signed a treaty with the Hittite empire, forming an alliance which promised 'peace for evermore'.

However when Ramesses died Egypt

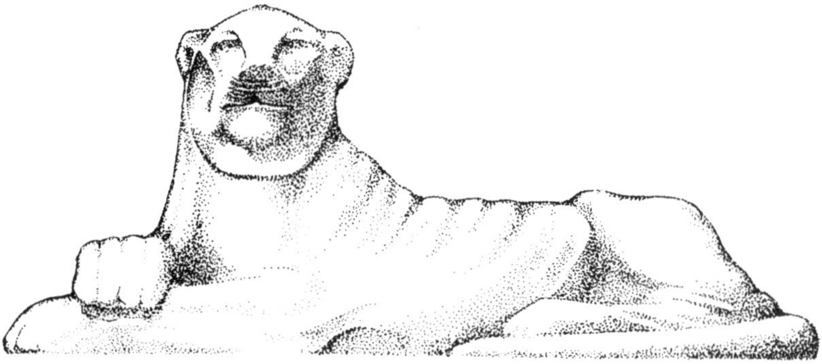

entered into a long period of gradual decline. Beyond its borders great changes were taking place. The power of the Hittites had diminished and the Minoan civilization on the island of Crete was destroyed about the year 1400 BCE by a tremendous earthquake. Great movements of people in Europe were causing ripples of instability. As the displaced tribes moved into coastal districts around the Mediterranean the local populations were forced out. These 'sea peoples', as they were known by the Egyptians, joined with the Libyans to attack Egypt's borders.

Ramesses III, the founder the Twentieth Dynasty, had therefore to fight constantly to protect his borders. Unrest abroad continued, the Hittite Empire finally collapsed and Troy fell. Crop failure in Egypt lead to famine, and tomb robbing proliferated. Finally Egypt was invaded by the sea peoples, however with the aid of Libyan mercenaries Ramesses III eventually defeated them in a battle fought on both land and sea.

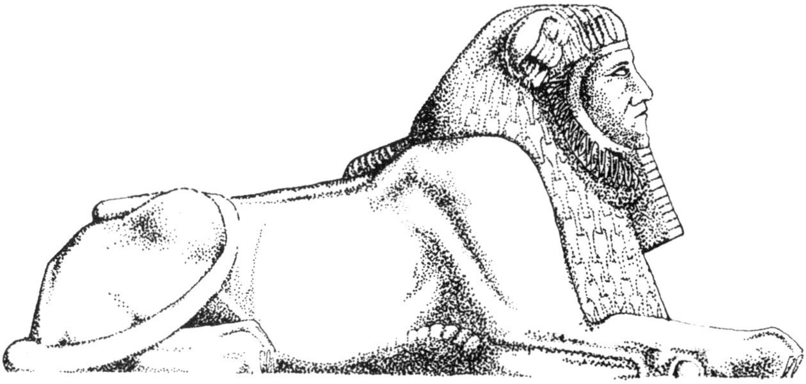

The Late Dynastic Period

With the fall of the Twentieth Dynasty about 1080 BCE Nubia broke from Egyptian control and Egypt itself was divided into two parts. The kings of the Twenty-first Dynasty ruled from Tanis, whilst the priests of Amun governed from Thebes. Although divided, Egypt was reasonably stable, and marriages between the sons and daughters of the leaders of the two ruling parties were common. During this time the priests reburied many mummies of dead kings in a tomb near Deir el Bahri to ensure their safety from grave robbers.

Sheshonk, a descendant of the Libyan mercenaries, was the first king of the Twenty-second Dynasty. He made Heracleopolis his capital and it was he who sacked Jerusalem and plundered the temple of Solomon. At this time the kings wrested power once more from the priests of Amun and ruled over the whole of the land.

In 730 BCE the Nubian King Plankhy took Egypt. Under his rule the arts flourished and new temples were built, although not to previous standards. As Egypt was now a weak military power, the king attempted to bring his influence to bear upon neighbouring countries by the use of political intrigue and bribes of Nubian gold. The Assyrian empire retaliated against this interference by occupying Memphis and Thebes, forcing the Nubians out of Egypt.

The Assyrians had problems elsewhere in their empire however, and so left Egypt under control of 12 trusted Egyptian princes. One of these, Psammetichus, took overall control and, raising an army of mercenaries, drove the remaining

Assyrians from Egypt. Later he built up a fine navy and merchant fleet. Manning his ships with Phoenician sailors, he dominated the Mediterranean. He vigorously promoted trade, inviting foreigners of all countries to settle in Egypt and providing them with privileges at the expense of the native Egyptians.

Corn was exported on a large scale, and this, with other trade income, enabled Egypt to re-establish some of her former glory. During this time a grand engineering project was begun to build a canal from the Nile to the Red Sea.

Interest in the past grew, and art attempted to revive the old styles, but in doing so it became imitative and lacking in originality. Nationalism also rose as the native population grew alarmed at the increase in the number of foreigners settling in Egypt. This lead to a state of anarchy and eventually to civil war.

With Egypt in turmoil the Persians had no difficulty in conquering the country in 525 BCE. Their king, Cambryses, became the first ruler of the Twenty-seventh Dynasty. An armed rebellion took place in 486 BCE, but it was swiftly subdued by the Persian King Xerxes.

During the Twenty-eighth to the Thirtieth Dynasties Egypt was once again independent, however it was conquered again in 343 BCE by the Persian King Artaxerxes III who formed the Thirty-first Dynasty.

The Ptolomaic Period

In 332 BCE Egypt was conquered by Alexander the Great and became part of the Macedonian Empire. Following Alexander's death the empire was divided amongst his generals, with Egypt falling to a man named Ptolomy.

The Macedonians went further than before in exploiting the Egyptian people to the benefit of foreigners. All land was confiscated by the crown with no form of compensation being offered. People were forced to work for the king on land they had once owned themselves. They had little freedom, and were taxed heavily. Even the type of crop to be grown was regulated by the central government, and prices were fixed by the state. Strikes by workers were bloodily suppressed by the authorities and the leaders executed. Marriages between Egyptian natives and foreigners was also strongly discouraged. Many Egyptians, disheartened by conditions in Egypt, left the banks of the Nile to live as hermits in the desert, forming communities similar to those of later Christian monastics.

During this period Egypt was ruled by 15 kings, all named Ptolomy. Despite their oppression of the Egyptian people, these rulers assumed Egyptian dress and followed the native customs. Temples were allowed to flourish, buildings were repaired and new temples constructed. The renowned library and museum at Alexandria were founded, and the city became the intellectual centre of the world. Here scholars assembled to pursue studies in all subjects and every branch of learning. Their work covered many fields of knowledge, including mathematics, medicine, magic, philosophy, astrology and astronomy. The store of ancient manuscripts was the greatest the world has ever known.

This period ended with Egypt's last and perhaps most famous queen, Cleopatra. In 30 BCE Egypt fell to the Romans.

The Gods

The Ancient Egyptians had a vast number of gods and goddesses. Some of them are well known to us, others are merely names mentioned perhaps only once in all the ancient writings that survive. Of those we know many have the heads of animals, reflecting their origin as simple animal fetishes, while others are human in form and only distinguishable from each other by their unique and often highly symbolic head-dresses. Each deity had his or her own position within the cults of Egypt.

As with all religions, beliefs changed over the years and from place to place. Originally in the predynastic period, each tribe had its own simple gods and beliefs. As time passed these became more complex and from interaction with other tribes and the introduction of new concepts, they took on new forms. When the tribes eventually settled in one place, one might for a time dominate the others, and the beliefs of the dominant chief would be promoted at the expense of the lesser tribes. This practice continued into dynastic times. The king would raise his own local god to that of main deity in the state religion, moving previous holders of that position to one side. Eventually there were a number of major gods whose cults were known throughout the whole of Egypt, and who were subject to the chief state god of the king.

In each of the main cult centres such as Thebes, Hermopolis, Heliopolis and Memphis, the priests sought to further their interests by vigorously promoting their own gods. This usually took the form of one group claiming that their chief god was the father of one or more of the other chief gods. At other times it was announced that two apparently individual gods were in fact the same deity worshipped under different names. It was in this way Ra became associated with Atum, eventually becoming Atum-Ra.

At first sight there appears to be many paradoxes in the religion of the Ancient Egyptians, of which two examples might be mentioned. Firstly as time progressed each of the major cult centres claimed that its chief god was solely responsible for the creation of the universe, giving rise to several independent creation myths. Secondly the priests throughout various parts of Egypt all pronounced that the dismembered head of Osiris was buried in their temple. But the mind of the Ancient Egyptian was such that these contradictions—and many more—were accepted without conflict. The king was happy to call himself the son of Ra, Atum *and* Horus, as he personified the sun and all were solar gods. As new concepts arose the old beliefs were never cast aside.

As the myths and attributes of the gods developed, their roles and relationships changed. For example, the agricultural deity Osiris, whose birth and death corresponded with the sowing and gathering of the harvest, came to be considered to be the supreme god of the dead. This in turn led Anubis, who had previously held that rank, to be demoted and made the son and assistant of Osiris.

As some gods rose to become official gods of the state others remained the gods of the people. This gave rise to the two distinct levels of religion within Egyptian society: that of the king or state and that of the individual. The two existed side by side in harmony, as the various minor deities worshipped by the people were believed to be local manifestations of either the overall state god or a god of one of the major cults.

Worship in the temples was reserved for the pharaoh (who was considered to be a god himself), and the priests who acted as his deputies. Within the temple the priests performed their religious rituals throughout the year, ceremonially enacting the god's life. The priests of Ra, for example, held three main services each day. At dawn they would celebrate the birth of the sun, at midday they rejoiced at his great strength, whilst with the fall of dusk they lamented his death.

At the great festivals of the major deities the image of the god would be carried out of the temple. It might be paraded around the local fields to confer prosperity upon the land, or alternatively taken to visit the temple of another god.

The ordinary people, although they might take part in ceremonial processions or enter the outer areas of the temple, were not admitted to the inner sanctum. However they did worship their own god at personal shrines that they often built themselves.

The gods of Egypt thus played a fundamental and crucial part in the lives of all its people. From pharaoh to peasant, each had a god corresponding to his place in society.

Amun

The god Amun is known to have been worshipped around the year 2000 BCE in the Fourth Nome of Upper Egypt. At this time he was only a minor fertility deity but within 150 years he had replaced the god Montu, a god of war, as the major deity of the district.

An unusual species of sheep was native to this part of Egypt and found nowhere else. The rams stood apart from other types of sheep, being distinguished by their especially large curving horns. This animal became the symbol of Amun, although he is never shown in Egyptian art as a ram or with a ram's head. As it was considered sacred to him, a living ram was kept in his temple. Amun's usual visual form in painting and sculpture was as a man wearing a cap upon which was the disc of the sun surmounted by two tall plumes.

The goose was a second creature also associated with fertility and sacred to Amun and a goose was kept in the enclosure of the temple.

In time Amun's sphere of influence changed. Once primarily a god of fertility in animals, he became a god of agriculture and was responsible for abundant crops and prosperity. As his popularity increased the pharaohs chose him as their own personal god, and as a result of their influence he became a solar god.

Originally in predynastic times he was the god of the wind, and his name means 'hidden' or 'invisible one'. Part of the rites of Amun involved concealing his shrine with a shroud. Linked to this idea of invisibility is another of his titles: 'he who abides in all things', confirming the belief that he was the very soul or 'ba' of the universe itself.

During the Middle Kingdom a temple was raised in Amun's honour at a town in the Eleventh Nome called Waset. The town and Amun grew together in importance until Waset was generally known as the city of Amun, or more simply The City. The place is referred to in the Bible, and given the names No Amun and No, meaning 'city of Amun' and 'city' respectively.

The Greeks compared Amun with Zeus, their chief god, and called Waset Diospolis, 'city of Zeus' or 'city of god'. Later this city of Amun became known as Thebes and it was here at the beginning of the Fourteenth Dynasty that King Amunemhat (meaning 'Amun is supreme') founded a temple of Amun. When the temple fell into disuse, debris and sand accumulated around the buildings to such an extent that only the upper windows of the main structures remained visible, thus inspiring the local Arabs to name the place 'town of windows', or, in Arabic, Karnak.

The prosperity of Thebes declined over the years following the Twelfth Dynasty, but with the dawn of the Eighteenth Dynasty its fortunes once again began to rise. Ahmose, a king of that Dynasty, made Thebes the capital of Egypt and the centre of the Egyptian empire, a meeting place for the cultures and beliefs of citizens of far

distant countries. From Thebes the cult of Amun spread out of Egypt to all points of the empire. By the time of the rulership of Thothmes III (1504-1450 BCE), Amun had become the major deity of the then civilized world and was acknowledged in all parts as the king of the gods.

As the power of Amun spread, his priests proclaimed him the creator of the universe, formulating complex legends describing how he had performed the act of creation in Thebes itself. Amun, they said, was the lord of time, who creates the years, governs the months and rules the nights and days. His followers claimed him to be a more powerful manifestation of the mighty god Ra and named him Amun-Ra.

The supporters of the other gods, including those of the eclipsed Ra, grew alarmed at the power that the priesthood of Amun was amassing. Eventually they rebelled, seeking to restore the old order. Although they did have some limited success the revolution was short-lived, and with his return to power Amun's popularity climbed to even greater heights. Of course as his popularity increased so did the fortunes of his priesthood and temples. By the year 1160 BCE approximately one fifth of the population of Egypt, along with one third of the arable land and three quarters of all the wealth of Egypt belonged to the temple of Amun-Ra at Thebes. Consequently the temple expanded: the vast complex of sacred buildings contained over 22 major shrines, the sacred enclosure covered an area of 1.25 square km and the main temple itself was over 1.5 km in length.

With all this power and wealth, Thebes became a semi-independent state within Egypt, ruled by the priests of Amun. Eventually this office became hereditary. Only with the beginning of the Twenty-second Dynasty about 935 BCE did Thebes once again start to become a true part of Egypt, and then the process of assimilation took almost two centuries.

Amun in his other aspect, that of the god of warfare, directed the king in his actions against the enemies of Egypt. The planning of the many campaigns of conquest was credited to him: he was the essential divine inspiration behind Egypt's successful strategies.

Although by the later period Amun had become primarily the god of the ruling monarch, the ordinary Egyptian still had access to him. By visiting the special temple of 'Amun who hears all prayers' a suppliant could ask the god for aid, and by leaving a small stele (an inscribed stone tablet) at its gate he could be sure that he would consider his request.

Within Amun's temple at Thebes a ritual boat named Woserhat was kept. It was richly made and decorated with great ram's heads covered in gold. Upon its deck an image of the god was positioned and during the festivals of Amun it would be ceremonially paraded before his worshippers.

Worship of Amun was linked with that of the god Min, who had a temple facing that of Amun on the opposite bank of the Nile at Thebes. As a result of this relationship Amun was at times depicted in Min's ithyphallic pose with his hand raised above his head holding a whip.

Incense played an important part in the rituals of Amun and tear-drops of the purest frankincense were thought to be formed from his perspiration. In his temple elaborate processional walk ways were flanked by rows of ram-headed sphinxes.

The pharaohs who supported Amun promoted the belief that he was their father by divine marriage with their earthly mother. In this way they identified the kingship with the god and so gained the full support of his priesthood. So important were the links between the cult of Amun and the rulers of Egypt that the highest officers in the priesthood were members of the king's family or high-ranking nobles. Later, in the form of Jupiter Ammon, Amun was worshipped into classical times. Even Alexander the Great felt the need to visit his temple at Thebes to obtain Amun's divine consent to rule his newly-conquered province, Egypt.

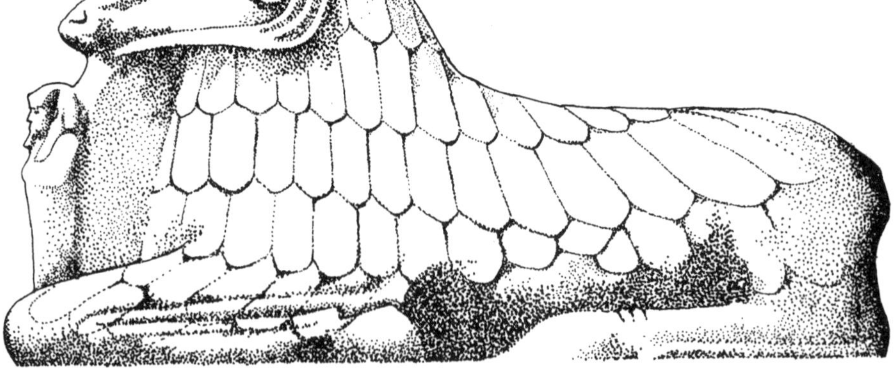

Anubis

For many centuries Anubis was the main god of the dead. Later, when the role of Osiris changed from god of vegetation to that of god of the dead, he became superior to Anubis. Anubis, however, retained an important part in the funeral rights and was considered to be the son of Osiris and Nephthys. It was Anubis, aided by his mother and aunt, the goddesses Nephthys and Isis, who embalmed the murdered Osiris's body, and he who devised the method of wrapping the body in bandages and formulated the embalming oils.

Anubis is shown in Egyptian art either as a jackal or as a man with a jackal's head. However the colouring is not the natural colour of the animal but a symbolic black, perhaps representing rebirth, or possibly recalling the colour assumed by the skin following treatment with natron and the other resins during the process of mummification.

In Ancient Egypt the necropolis or cemetery would be situated in the desert to the west of the settlement to which it was attached. This was for three reasons: firstly, by placing the cemetery in the desert essential good farming land was not lost, secondly, as good farming land symbolized life, so the desert came to represent death and was a natural place to house the dead, and thirdly, the gate or entrance to the realm of the dead was believed to lie in the west, as Ra in the form of the setting sun was seen to die there each day, slowly descending into the underworld. On edge of the desert the jackal lived, scavenging what he could from the communities and frequenting the cemeteries which lay within his natural habitat. So it was inevitable that this animal should become associated with the dead.

One of the main areas for the worship of Anubis was the Seventeenth Nome of Upper Egypt, the capital of which the Greeks named Cynopolis, 'the city of the dogs'.

As the embalmer of Osiris, Anubis became the patron of all embalmers. One of his titles was 'lord of the divine pavilion', referring to the building within each temple complex where mummification was

carried out. In his early history the rites of Anubis were the domain of the king alone, but as time passed he became the god of death for all members of the community.

On passing from this life to the next, the deceased was judged to test his worthiness to enter the afterlife. As part of this test Anubis took the deceased's heart and weighed it upon his scales against a feather, the symbol of Ma'at, goddess of truth. Nearby stood Thoth, the celestial scribe, recording the findings of the trial. Then the deceased stood before each of the 42 assembled gods, and to each in turn he denied that he had committed any of the 42 sins. Instructions for the soul on the correct way to present this negative confession were painted on the inside of the tomb and form Chapter 125 of *The Book of the Dead.*

If the deceased passed the test he was pronounced 'true of voice' or 'justified', and taken by Horus to the presence of Osiris, who upon his throne, flanked by Isis and Nephthys, granted him access to the afterlife.

However, for those who failed the judgement, punishment was severe. Outside the hall of judgement the monster Beby 'the destroyer' lay waiting to consume them. Beby was a composite creature with the head of a crocodile, the body of a lion and the rear of a hippopotamus.

Related to Anubis was the god Wapwawet. He was also a god of the dead, resembling Anubis in several ways. Both gods were dog-headed but where Anubis was shown with a black head, that of Wapwawet was white. It is probable that his head was that of a wolf, for his cult centre in the Thirteenth Nome of Upper Egypt was called by the Greeks Lykopolis—'the wolf city'.

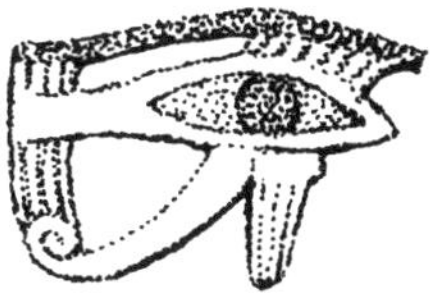

Aten

In the fourteenth century BCE, King Akhenaten ruled Egypt for some 17 years. During this time he broke completely away from the traditions that had existed unchanged for over a thousand years before him. In both religion and in art his ideas were revolutionary. Originally named Amenhotep IV, 'Amun is satisfied', he changed this to Akhenaten, 'the glorious spirit of Aten', in the fifth year of his reign, and adopted Aten as the god of all Egypt and its empire, which at that date covered practically all of the civilized world.

In the following year he and his wife, Nefetiti, built a new capital from which to rule the empire at a place between Memphis and Thebes called Akhetaten, 'the horizon of Aten'.

To promote the worship of the sun god Aten, the king began by closing the temples of rival gods, even those under the control of the powerful priests of Amun. Then he created a new trinity, consisting of Ra the creator god, Aten, who as the sun was visible to man, and himself, Akhenaten, the earthly manifestation of the god. He decreed that he should be regarded as both the father and the embodiment of Ra and Aten.

Monotheism such as Akhenaten advocated had always been implicit within Egyptian religion. Each individual worshipper viewed the great state god of the period as merely a distant personification of his own more personal and intimate local deity. The Ancient Egyptian was therefore quite comfortable assimilating his private beliefs with those of the state religion, and happy to acknowledge the god of the ruling classes as meaningful, if distant, to his own spiritual well-being. Prior to Akhenaten the kings had simply placed their own favoured god above the rest, usually by making him equal or superior to the prevailing highest god. It then followed that all the secondary gods and goddesses became subservient to the newly-elevated deity. This process had gone on for as long as Egypt had been a civilized nation, and the people were content to follow the system, for as they still had their own local and personal

gods, the change of the state god did little to affect their individual lives or beliefs.

However Akhenaten went further than previous rulers. In adapting religion to suit his purposes, he proscribed the worship of secondary deities, declaring them to be false. He removed Osiris and the other gods from the official state religion, but put nothing in their place. By banning all the other deities Akhenaten not only effectively severed the only link that the people would have had with his god Aten, but he denied them a personal religion of any description. The people were left with the choice of accepting his distant and highly conceptual monotheism or else living in a state of spiritual starvation. As a result his policies were not popular and even within his own lifetime the supremacy of Aten began to fade.

Akhenaten's effect upon art was equally profound. Under his rule we find little of the idealized forms that typify the Egyptian style. Instead the human figure is represented in a much more naturalistic manner. The king himself is portrayed with thin weak arms and a bulging paunch, and the royal family are shown in much less formal situations that the artist had ever been permitted or had even desired to show them before.

However even within this apparent artistic freedom new conventions are evident. The realistic approach of the painters towards Akhenaten

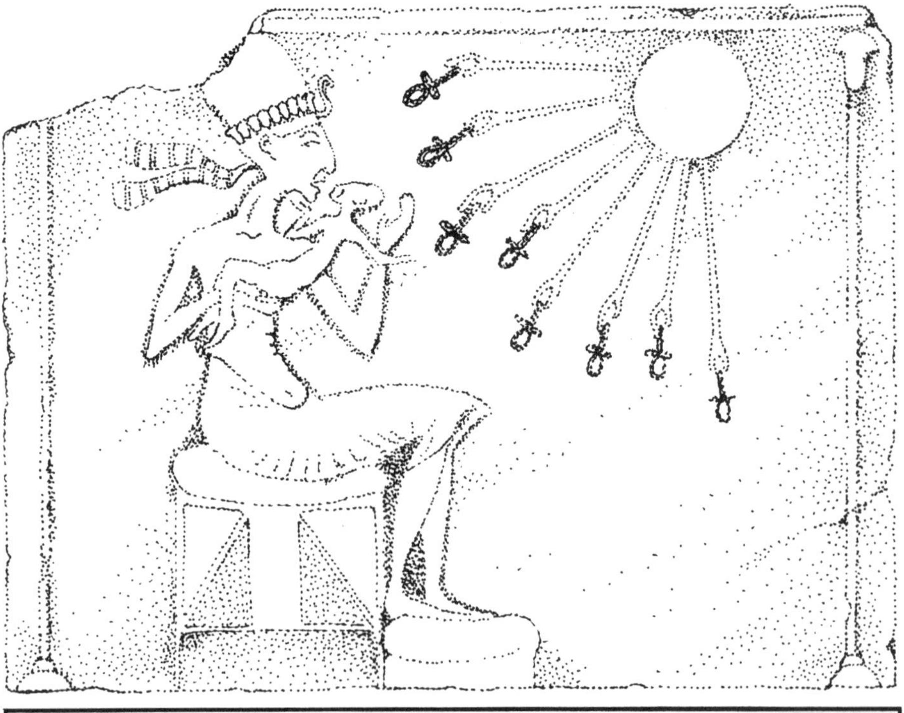

himself is diminished when one comes to other figures represented by the artists. It may be true that Akhenaten was overweight with spindly arms and legs but all the other figures of that time are treated in a similar fashion, suggesting that the artist was not as free as it may at first appear!

Aten was not an invention of Akhenaten, but has his origins in the remote past. The word 'aten' could originally be used to refer to any disc-shaped object, whether it was a mirror or the moon. But as most solar gods were at some time identified with the image of the solar disc and so with the word 'aten', as early as 2000 BCE the word implied divinity.

In both painting and sculpture, Aten was not represented as the other gods were, that is by animal, anthropomorphic or human form, but was shown instead as the sun disc. Indeed it was thought that the disc of the sun observed every day crossing the heavens from west to east was the god Aten himself. Later the sun disc was shown emanating rays which terminated in small hands, many of which held ankhs, representing the beneficial, life-giving powers of Aten.

Akhenaten's building programme began with the construction of a temple to Aten outside the perimeter wall of the sacred temple of Amun. It was erected immediately to the east, thus depriving Amun of the first rays of the sun each morning. Following the king's reign this temple was

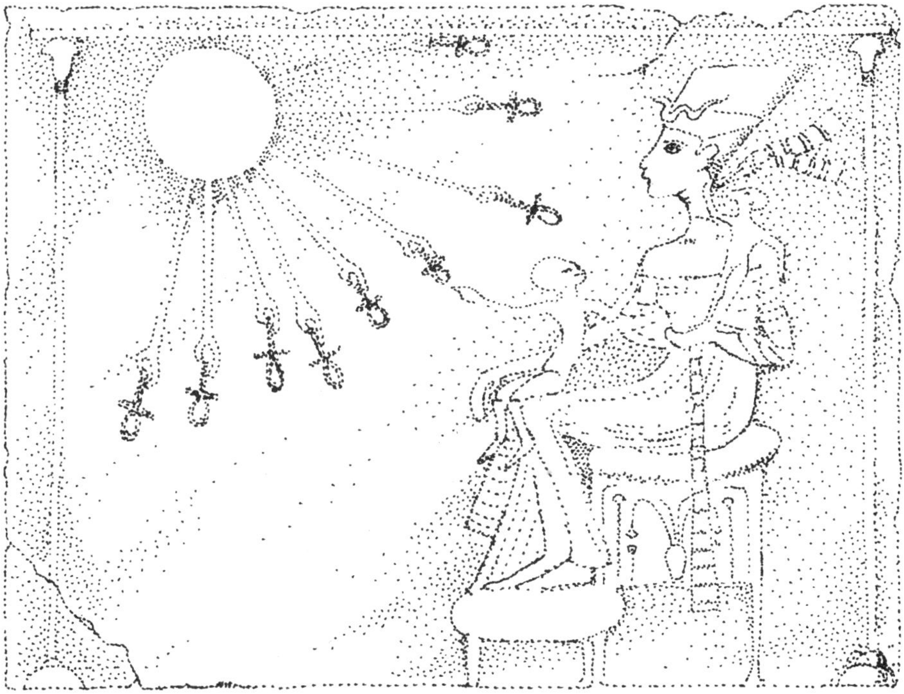

dismantled stone by stone, many of them being used in the construction of other projects in the area. The inscriptions upon them provide us with a wealth of information about the period. Other information is scarce due to the work of those following Akhenaten, who tried to eradicate not only his work but his very name from Egypt.

It was a tradition that temples in Egypt were constructed upon the site of earlier places of worship and naturally some of the attributes of the preceding deities were absorbed by the god of the new temple. So in choosing to build on a virgin site Akhenaten again cut his links with the past in his desire to form a religion untainted by those which had gone before.

The design of Aten's temples was based upon the even then ancient temples of the sun. Unlike the more recent temples of Egypt these buildings were constructed without roofs, thus permitting the entry of sunlight into the innermost sanctuaries.

Akhenaten declared himself the only priest of Aten, and devised the rituals of Aten himself, even to the composition of the hymns to be sung at the god's festivals. These hymns marked an important departure from those of earlier periods, in that they contained no allusions to other Egyptian gods or their associated myths. Consequently they both divorced Aten from any direct association with previous gods, setting him apart from and above all others, and they could be understood not only by the Egyptians but also by those outside Egypt. The message of the hymns was that all men were equally the sons of Aten.

The temples of other gods were closed and defiled, and their wealth confiscated and used to further the glory of Aten.

Statues were smashed and holy names erased from inscriptions on the walls. This was even carried to the extent of removing the name of Amenhotep III, Akhenaten's father.

But following the death of Akhenaten, reversal to the old ways was rapid. Even the king's son and successor rejected his father's changes and restored the cult of Amun as the state religion. He changed his own name, given to him by Akhenaten, from Tutankhaten, meaning 'living image of Aten' to Tutankhamun, 'living image of Amun'.

In the tomb of Ay, Akhenaten's vizier, a hymn to Aten has been discovered, carved into the walls. It describes the uniqueness of the god and separates him from all others, telling how he alone created all things, transmitting his beneficence to the earth in the form of rays. It reminds the reader that when he passes from the sky at the end of the day and darkness falls there comes a time of fear and death, when all that is evil is permitted to walk the earth unchecked. All that is good and orderly, we are told, prospers under the will of Aten. He cares for all things; nothing is too small or insignificant to be of concern to him. He provides sustenance to all things. It was he who divided humanity into its various races and colours, giving them their individual languages.

The hymn closes by stating that Akhenaten 'alone' has the true knowledge of Aten, denying the individual the right of speculating upon the nature of the god, and permitting only the acceptance of the authorized view. Such was the oppressive nature of the monotheism of Akhenaten.

Atum

Atum was a sun god and, according to the priests of his cult, creator of the universe. His name is derived from a word that meant both 'to be complete' and 'to make an end of'. This concept is clearly seen in his position as a father of the gods. He was the original god of Heliopolis, preceding Ra, but even from the earliest times the two gods were closely identified with each other. They are linked in legend, and many similarities exist in the stories associated with them, to the point where their names may be considered to be interchangeable. Sometimes Atum represented the sun in the evening while Ra was the sun in the morning

In sacred art Atum is shown wearing the double crown of united Egypt and, as the creator, he carries an ankh, the symbol of life.

Several animals were associated with Atum, including the lion, bull, lizard, ichneumon (a type of mongoose), and snake. In the snake form Atum represents the concept of the end of the universe, following which only he and Osiris survive. *The Book of the Dead* speaks of a time when the waters of Nun will rise up and engulf the earth, consuming both men and gods, and leaving only Osiris and Atum living on in the form of serpents.

Bast

Bast or Bastet was originally a lion goddess, but over the years as her cult developed she became more associated with the cat and was considered to be the gentler counterpart of the lion goddess Sekhmet.

Cats were much loved by the Egyptians. Illustrations on papyrus show them sitting beneath chairs waiting for treats from the feast table, and appearing in hunting scenes where they assist their masters, having being trained to retrieve birds brought down from the sky by a throwing stick.

The ancient Egyptian word for cat was 'miw', which obviously reflects an attempt to imitate the voice of the cat itself. Such was the popularity of the cat that small girls were affectionately called 'miw-sheri', meaning literally 'little cat' or 'kitten'.

Cats could be observed skilfully hunting and catching snakes, which had special relevance for the Egyptians in that in addition to being dangerous to man the snake was the symbol of Apophis, the demonic enemy of the sun god Ra. So cats became animals sacred to the solar deity, and in the markings upon cats' heads the Egyptians saw an image of the scarab beetle, symbol of the rising sun. Also the eyes of the cat were seen to change with movement of the sun. When the sun was at its strongest cats' eyes would be almost completely golden, but when the sun set and darkness fell their pupils would open and the eyes too would become as black as the night sky.

Figures of cats were offered to Bast by her followers to win her favour and thousands of mummified cats were buried in the special cemeteries of Bubastis, 'house of Bast'.

Bast is shown on wall paintings as a cat-headed woman. In one hand she holds either a sistrum, a kind of musical rattle more commonly associated with the goddess Hathor, or an aegis, in her other hand she carries a basket. She is often confused by the Egyptians, possibly intentionally, with Sekhmet, and was therefore considered to be the wife of Ptah. Her fame lasted throughout the whole of the Egyptian period, but her popularity rose to a peak in the fourth century BCE. She had a son, the lion-headed god Mihos, the 'savage faced' lion god, 'Lord of Slaughter'.

As a sun goddess Bast was the goddess of plenty and the mistress of pleasure. The celebrations of her orgiastic festivals were renowned for being the most lavish of all the gods of Egypt. During these festivals it was forbidden to hunt lions for fear of suffering her wrath.

To her followers Bast was a virgin goddess, (despite the events occurring at her festivals and being the patroness of women and children) and was associated by the Greeks with their virgin goddess Artemis.

In other myths Bast is associated with the moon rather than the sun and is referred to as the eye of the moon, the twin of Horus or the eye of the sun. Her popularity extended through the Greek period and the Romans took her cult to Europe, where she was worshipped in various places, Rome and Pompeii amongst them.

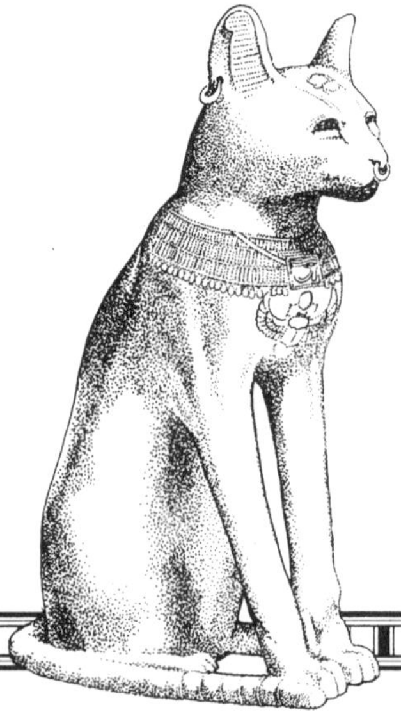

Hapi

The great god of the Nile was called Hapi. In sacred art he is shown as an overweight man, symbolizing abundance, with the breasts of a woman, representing the life-giving properties of the river. Often he holds before him a tray of offerings, the gifts of the Nile. He wears a crown of riverside plants, the lotus of Upper Nile and the papyrus of the Lower Nile. Hapi had a wife in both the north and the south of the country—these were the personifications of the river banks. He was also the patron god of fish and marsh birds.

Hapi's home was reputed to be in a cave on the island of Bigehin on the Nile. He was worshipped at Adu, known to the Greeks as Elephantine, and was closely associated with the god Khnum.

Although he represented the waters of the Nile, Hapi does not appear to have been held responsible for the inundation, as this was the province of more powerful gods.

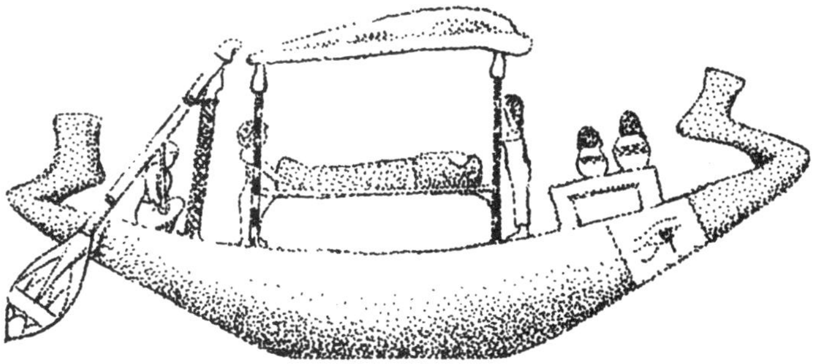

Hathor

Hathor' was the Hellenic form of the name Athyr, whom the Greeks identified with their own goddess Aphrodite. Her name can be translated as 'the dwelling [or house] of Horus', for it was thought that Horus the sun god came to rest each evening on her breast before being reborn with the awakening dawn.

Other sources tell of Hathor being the celestial cow who gave birth to the universe and all that it contains. She is often represented either in the form of a cow or with some bovine attribute such as a cow's head, horns on her head-dress or cow's ears.

Throughout the Egyptian period Hathor was considered to be the goddess of many things, some of which were at times contradictory. She presided over both heaven and the underworld, she was a moon goddess, a sky goddess and even a sun goddess, and as the dwelling of Horus she represented both the eastern and western horizons. As a mother goddess she was confused with Nut and Isis. But her main attributes reveal her to have been a moon goddess, and her head-dress often consists of a pair of horns (an ancient lunar symbol) with the moon's disc between them. She is also often depicted being carried upon a boat, as water was her element.

The myths make it clear that she was both a giver and taker of life, and was linked to the cycles of agriculture as goddess of moisture and vegetation. In the underworld the souls of the dead hung from the branches of palm and sycamore trees, and she would walk amongst them, providing them with thirst-quenching water. Her role of caring for the dead led her to be called the Queen of the West, where the dead were believed to reside. (With Renutet she kept a protective watch over the Theban necropolis.)

According to *The Book of the Dead,* when the soul arrived at the entrance to the underworld it would be greeted by Hathor in the form of a cow. Those who asked for her aid using the correct ritual phrases could expect to be carried on their way upon her back.

She was the goddess of joy and love, of music, dance and song. Her temple at Dendera was the house of intoxication and enjoyment. Hathor is also linked with the sistrum, which was used in her rituals and with which she would confer her blessings.

The association of joy and intoxication on one hand and death and the underworld on the other suggests that her rituals involved some kind of shamanistic practices. Divine madness freed her priests or followers from the mundane world, and with the correct training they were able to move onto other planes and walk with the gods.

Hathor's following was widespread and her shrines extremely numerous, for as time passed she gradually absorbed the attributes of many local or minor goddesses. Her main cult centre was at Dendera, where she was worshipped along with her husband, Horus of Edfu. Their son was Ihy or Ahy, the sistrum player.

Hathor was also linked with the star Sirius, which rises just before dawn on the first day of the month of Thoth. This day was especially significant to the followers of Hathor, as it was the day of the festival celebrating her birth.

Sekhmet-Hathor

When the gods still lived upon the earth, the greatest of them, the creator of all things and king of the gods was Ra. He ruled over mankind and was obeyed by all.

As time passed, however, he grew old and those who had once paid him homage and revered him began to mock him openly. They disdainfully compared his bones to silver, his flesh to gold and his hair to lapis lazuli. Ra grew wrathful, and anger filled his heart when he heard their irreverent voices and the rebellious words upon their lips. He assembled the gods together, secretly hidden from the eyes of men, deep within the innermost confines of his temple at Heliopolis.

Ra turned to Nun, his father, the oldest and wisest of the gods and asked for his advice and guidance. Should he destroy humanity as he so desired? Nun agreed that the rebellious people should be punished for their lack of reverence, instructing Ra to turn his eye upon them that they might perish for their sins.

But when Ra attempted to do so, the people, wise to his intent, ran hastily from his gaze and fled into the desert, concealing themselves amongst the rocky hills of the vast uninhabited regions. Observing their escape, Ra devised a new plan. He gave his powerful eye to the goddess Hathor, who, assuming the lion form of

Sekhmet, walked through the desert amongst them, mercilessly slaying all she found. When he saw the carnage and destruction, however, Ra grew saddened, his anger passed from him, and at length he wished that those who had escaped destruction should be forgiven and allowed to live in peace.

After her day of killing Sekhmet-Hathor spent the whole night revelling in the blood of her victims, wading in the gore of the slain. Ra watched her in her blind ecstasy and he grew fearful that with the coming dawn she would once again go forth and this time slay the entire remainder of the human race. So, calling for the swiftest of his messengers, he commanded that they should go with haste and bring unto him a great quantity of mandrakes from Elephantine. On their return, the mandrakes were beaten and ground, some of the blood of the slaughter was added and finally the essence was mixed with beer made of barley. The quantity was such that 7,000 jars were filled.

Just as the first rays of dawn spread across the eastern sky, the jars were taken to the place where the goddess would begin to resume her work, and there the contents were poured upon the earth.

When Sekhmet-Hathor came to the place where the red beer flooded the earth, turning the ground black, she stopped and looked within its reflecting surface. So pleased was she with the sight of her reflection that she forgot her task and drank deeply of the rich liquid. Soon she became so intoxicated that she was unable to further harm mankind.

The men crept silently from their places of concealment and back to their homes where they lived again respectfully under the rule of Ra.

Horus

There were two gods who bore the name Horus: the first was a solar deity and brother of Set, the second the child of Osiris and Isis. However in later times the Egyptians appear to have been either unable or unwilling to distinguish between the two, and the offspring of Osiris and Isis was also considered to be a sun god, thus the two gods became one.

The name Horus is a Latinized form of the Greek 'Hores' which in turn is derived from the Egyptian 'Hor'. The origin of this name may come from the same root as the Egyptian word for 'high' or 'far away'.

Horus was represented either as a falcon or a falcon-headed man. His two eyes symbolized the two heavenly bodies, the sun and the moon, with the right eye being the sun and the left the moon. However the phrase 'the eye of Horus' usually refers to the moon. It was this eye that was lost

to Set and later, after being recovered, presented to Osiris to aid him in his resurrection.

The four sons of Horus, Imset, Qebehsenuf, Duamuttef and Hapi, acted as guides to the dead. They represented the cardinal points and were found either pictorially or by name on each of the four sides of the coffin. They protected the body from hunger and thirst and also watched over the internal organs of the deceased, which were removed from the body during mummification and held in canopic jars, each of which bore a moulded head of one of the sons.

The falcon was sacred to Horus from the earliest times and the image of a falcon on its perch became the hieroglyphic symbol representing the word 'god'. Many sanctuaries were dedicated to him, and in each one his priests appear to have developed their own collection of myths associated with the god. So varied did these become that at first glance it would appear that we have over a dozen gods bearing the name Horus, some of which are provided below.

Haroeris

Worshipped at Letopolis and at Pharbocthos, Haroeris's name in Egyptian is Har-Wer, Horus 'the great' or 'elder'. To the priest of Letopolis he was also known as Horkenti Irti, 'Horus who rules the two eyes', whilst at Pharbocthos, he was Hor Marti, 'Horus of the two eyes'. His birth was celebrated when the sun and moon were in conjunction.

In the pyramid texts, illustrations show Ra the great sun god with his sons, Horus and Set, either side of him, Horus representing light and Set darkness. In the eternal battle between the two gods, Set rips out his brother's eye and is in return castrated by Horus. In later texts the battle is between Set and his nephew, Horus the son of Osiris and not Horus the Elder.

Harakhte

Harakhte meant 'the god on the horizon'. Horus was the first state god of Egypt, but in early times he appears to have become so confused with Ra that the two gods exchanged places, with Ra eventually becoming known as Ra-Harakhte.

Behdety or Bedhey

Behdety or Bedhey was worshipped at Behdety in Edfu. The myth linking Horus and Edfu tells of an occasion when Ra-Harakhte, who was with his army in Nubia, heard of a plot against him led by Set. Ra-Harakhte sailed down the Nile from Nubia to Edfu, where Set had assembled his demonic army, and commanded his son Horus to fight on his behalf against his enemy. This Horus did, rising up into the sky in the form of a fiery disc and flying over the land, slaying the demonic followers of Set wherever he found them. To commemorate his valuable service his father gave him the title Horus Behdety, Horus of Edfu.

Behdety was usually represented in the form of a winged sun disc and may be seen carved above temple gates and other places. He is also present in battle scenes where he flies protectively above the pharaoh in the form of a great falcon holding the ring of eternity.

Harmakhis

This is the Greek form of Hormakhet, 'Horus of the horizon'. Horus was the personification of the rising sun and thus also a symbol of resurrection. Harmakhis is the true name of the Sphinx, although it is carved in the image of King Kephren. The Sphinx faces directly to that point on the eastern horizon where the sun is first seen at the equinox and also acts as a guardian of the pyramid of the king.

Harsiesis

Harsiesis is the Greek form of Horsaiset, 'Horus the son of Isis'. He is the posthumous son of Osiris born to Isis on the floating island of Chemmis, situated in the marshes of the Delta near Buto. In his early youth he was known as Harpakhrad, 'the infant Horus' and was later known as Horus the Younger. In sculpture the young Harsiesis is shown dressed as a typical Egyptian child wearing no clothing but quantities of jewellery and baring the sidelock of youth.

Originally a minor god from Buto, as he became more popular Harsiesis gathered to himself all the attributes of the other forms of Horus. In the pyramid texts it is Harsiesis who performs the essential 'opening of the mouth' ceremony, a magical act which had the effect of restoring the dead king for his existence in the afterlife.

Later in his campaigns against Set, his father's murderer, he was known as Hartomes, 'Horus the Lancer', and by this time he had almost completely assumed the identity of Horus the Elder.

Isis

Isis is the Greek name of the goddess known to the Egyptians as 'Aset' or 'Eset'. The Greeks associated her with their earth goddesses Demeter and Hera and also the moon goddess Selene. She was one of the most popular of all Egyptian deities, and as time passed she began to assume and absorb the traits, functions and personalities of practically all the other goddesses. Her fame spread far, she was worshipped in Rome and the Romans carried her name throughout their empire.

Isis began as a local goddess in the north of Egypt, possibly in Perehbet, where a temple was later built and dedicated to her. As her following grew she became known as the wife of Osiris and, together with their son Horus, they became the most loved and respected gods of Egypt.

Assisting her husband in the task of civilizing the people of the Nile, Isis taught women the methods of grinding corn and showed them how to spin flax and weave cloth. She was skilled in the arts of healing and passed on her knowledge to her people. When Osiris left Egypt to spread the word of civilization to the rest of the world, she stayed behind, proving herself to be a great and just ruler while acting as his regent.

After Set had cut the body of Osiris into 14 pieces and cast them into the Nile, Isis, aided by Nephthys her sister, recovered all but one part. This was the phallus, which had been swallowed by a fish. Using her magic she skilfully brought the individual parts together and reformed the whole. Then, with the help of Anubis, the body was embalmed and Osiris was restored to eternal life.

Isis's knowledge of the magical arts was vast, but she constantly wished that it was greater. She was jealous of her grandfather Ra, the wisest and most practised of the gods in the ways of magic. With time he had become old and infirm. Isis watched him, considering ways in which she might learn the secret of his power, for he would never give it up of his own free will. Then she observed that saliva dribbled from his lip, and so decided on a plan of action. Secretly she collected some of this liquid and mixed it in her hands with the earth upon which Ra had walked. From the clay she fashioned a serpent then, using her magic, she transformed it into an arrow. When her task was completed she took the arrow and, voicing words of power, she secreted it at a crossroads where she knew Ra would pass the following day.

As dawn broke Ra, accompanied by other gods, walked his familiar road from horizon to horizon, eventually coming to the crossroads and the hidden magical

arrow. Sensing the great god's presence, the arrow suddenly sprang to life and plunged its serpent fangs deep into his leg.

Ra fell to the ground writhing in agony and babbled incoherently as the poison spread rapidly through his body. The other gods gathered around helpless, for it was beyond their understanding that the great and all-powerful Ra could be so afflicted. He was the father of the gods, he had created all things, and they could not comprehend how anything of his own making would harm him.

After a time Ra summoned the strength to beckon one of them to his side, then, speaking in a barely audible whisper, he told him that he feared for his life, adding that he had no idea what power could have caused his distress. He begged that the gods of magic should be summoned to restore him to health. None of these gods, however, knew how to help their lord—whichever way they tried they could not free him from the spell which so fearfully gripped his weakening body.

Then came Isis who immediately went up to Ra's side and whispered into his ear that she could free him from the magic if only he would reveal his true name to her, thereby giving her the secret of his magical power. After much thought, and urged by his suffering, Ra at last consented,

upon the condition that she should in turn permit his name to be told to none save her son Horus and that he should likewise keep it to himself until the end of time.

Initially Ra tried to trick Isis by giving her his titles and listing his feats and honours rather than his name. He said his name was 'creator of the heavens above and the earth below', he said that he was 'the one who made the waters flow and caused the air to move', he was 'lord of the horizons of dawn and dusk', 'father of the gods and master of the Nile', 'the origin of time', he was 'Khepri' in the morning, 'Ra' at noon and 'Atum' in the evening. But Isis rebuked him, telling him that he delayed his cure, for without his true name there was nothing that she could do to help him. So with deep reluctance the old god agreed and, concealing them both from the gaze of the other gods, Ra caused his name to move secretly from its place in his own heart to that of Isis. This done she cheerfully pronounced her magical formula and the poison began to ebb away from his painful body. Soon he was restored to health.

From that time forth, Isis was the most powerful of the gods and she had knowledge of all things.

The hieroglyph representing her name was a picture of a throne or seat. In Egyptian painting she is identified by wearing this symbol on her head. In later times she is occasionally shown bearing the solar disk upon her head supported by a pair of cow's horns and sometimes surmounted by two feathers borrowed from the goddess Hathor, with whom she later came to share some of her attributes. At other times she is shown with the protecting wings of the kite.

She was a universal goddess and was identified with Sothis (the Egyptian name of the star Sirius), which lies close to the constellation of Orion. The Egyptians later linked Orion with Osiris. Isis was also worshipped under the name Isothis.

Until the Thirtieth Dynasty Isis had no temples of her own, but a section of every temple in Egypt was set apart and dedicated in her name. During the Thirtieth Dynasty however, the ruler Nectaanebo II built a temple in her honour at Behbeit-el-Hagar in the eastern Delta. The temple was called the Iseum by the Greeks and there Isis and her husband Osiris and son Horus were worshipped continually until the sixth century CE.

Isis is often depicted as a mother suckling her young son Horus, which considering the supernatural conception of the divine child, cannot fail to suggest similar images of the later Christian period.

Khepri

The name Khepri has two interpretations: firstly 'scarab', the sacred beetle of Ancient Egypt, and secondly 'he who becomes'. Khepri was represented by a scarab in iconography and symbolized the dawning sun, which had just come into existence or been 'born' in the east. The Egyptians visualized this as the beetle pushing the sun across the morning sky. Images of the god also occur consisting of a human figure with a scarab in the place of a head.

It was believed that the scarab beetle was born from a ball of dung without recourse to the usual reproductive processes. As a result Khepri was equated with Atum, the self-creating sun god, and later with Ra.

Khepri's image is found in practically all the temples of Egypt because of his associations with the ever-powerful sun gods.

In the Middle Kingdom amulets in the form of scarabs became popular. Carved in the shape of the beetle, the underside was flat and could be inscribed with spells for good luck or magical symbols.

Khnum

Khnum was a god of fertility and creation. He was known as the potter god, for he is often shown in sacred painting in the act of modelling human figures upon a potter's wheel, each with its Ka or double alongside. As he created humanity he allotted each of them a period of time on earth, beyond which no man could live. His name means literally 'the moulder'.

In some myths it was Khnum who created the cosmic egg, having turned it upon his wheel. It was believed that he gave form to all things, creating both gods and men. But eventually Khnum became tired of endlessly spinning his wheel and he devised a new way to perpetuate life upon the earth. He broke up his wheel and placed a portion of it in all female creatures. From that time forth all living things had the power to reproduce without the need for his participation.

When translated by the Greeks Khnum became Khnoumis. He was originally shown as a man with a ram's head. His appearance was similar to that of Amun, but his horns were wavy as opposed to Amun's sweeping curves. A species of sheep possessing horns of this type was *Ouislongipes palaeoegypticos*. The animal is known to have become extinct about the beginning of the second millennium BCE, so Khnum's cult must have been well established long before this.

Khnum's main centre of worship was at Abu, the capital city of the Abu or Elephant Nome. The city was built upon an island in the Nile, and the myths of Khnum link him closely with the Nile. The annual inundation of the Nile was thought to begin in the sacred pool on the island of Abu.

The other members of the Elephantine triad were Anukis and Satis. Anukis, Khnum's first wife, may have originated in the Sudan, as she is shown wearing the feathers of the red parrot, a bird restricted to that area. His second wife was Satis, who was also his daughter by Anukis. Her name means 'she who runs like an arrow'. She is often shown holding a bow and arrow, and because of this the Greeks linked her with Hera. Later, perhaps because of the similarity of their names, Satis became linked with Sothis, the dog star. In this aspect she is shown with a star upon her head.

Khonsu

Khonsu was the adopted son of Amun and Mut, and became the third member of the Theban triad, replacing Montu. For some unknown reason the Greeks named him Hercules.

His usual form in Egyptian art is that of a young man or child, bound like a mummy, with the sidelock of youth, and a crescent and full moon upon his head. In his hands, which emerge from the bindings, he holds a crook and sceptre.

His name appears to be derived from a word meaning 'to cross over' or 'wanderer', suggesting that Khonsu means 'he who traverses', a fitting title for a moon god such as he.

In his capacity as lunar god he assisted Thoth, helping him to record the passing of time and also served as a healer of the sick and protector against evil spirits. In addition he was well practised as an exorcist. Evil spirits were often considered to be the source of an illness, so that physicians were by necessity wise in the ways of magic. It is reported that the sick were taken by their families and friends from all parts of Egypt to Khonsu's temple to be cured of their ills. For those who were unable to travel or lived in distant places, his statue was sent abroad, as it was believed that the presence of his image was all that was required to achieve a cure.

He was linked with Horus, the son of Osiris and Isis, perhaps because, like Horus, he was the child member of a triad, and so came to be depicted with a hawk's head. However as more befitting a lunar god the baboon, sacred to the moon, was also one of his animals.

Min

Min, an aspect of the god Amun, was one of the oldest of the Egyptian deities. His symbol was the thunder bolt and he was always shown as a man with an erect phallus. On rare occasions he has a lion's head. As a god of fertility and vegetation the Greeks associated him with their god Pan, but otherwise their cults were dissimilar. The town of Akhmis, where he was worshipped, was named Panopolis by the Greeks.

The cult of Min was one of the longest lasting and most widespread, being popular throughout the whole of Egypt in all periods. This was especially so in the cities of Gebtu and Kmentmin. In both these places he was worshipped in the form of a white bull.

The lettuce, because of its aphrodisiac properties, was closely associated with Min, and at the beginning of the harvest season, his image would be brought out from the temple into the fields. This formed the central part of the 'festival of the coming forth of Min', during in which the crops were blessed and gymnastic games were held in his honour.

Montu

Montu was a hawk-headed god, the solar god and god of war in Upper Egypt. Although he is mentioned in early texts it was not until the Eleventh Dynasty, when the kings from Iuny in the Fourth or the Sceptre Nome of Upper Egypt came to power, that he acquired any great following. These kings promoted the worship of Montu, for he was their own local god.

Montu was compared and equated with Ra, Amun and Horus, one of his many titles being 'Horus with the strong arm', and like Ra he traversed the heavens in a golden barque.

He was worshipped either as a man with a hawk's or a bull's head, or in the form of a complete bull, but in both these forms his head could be surmounted by the solar disc and two tall feathers. A sacred bull was in fact kept within his temple at Hermonthis in Iuny, and was known as the Bekh or Buchis bull. It was a beast of great strength and ferocity, whose coat was reputed to change colour with each hour of the day.

With the fall of the Eleventh Dynasty and the rise of the Twelfth, the cult of Montu lost its favour and he was eclipsed by the god Amun. However he still remained popular with the more warlike kings.

Mut

The goddess Mut was the wife of Amun and so was a sky goddess. Her name meant literally 'mother'. As the Greeks equated her husband with Zeus, the father of the gods, so she was compared with Hera, his wife.

In earliest times she was worshipped in the form of a vulture, the hieroglyph of her name being a picture of that bird, and in painting and sculpture she is usually shown wearing a head-dress in the form of a vulture. The relationship between motherhood and vultures is difficult for us to understand, but may stem from the vulture's habit of extending its wings to cover the young protectively whilst providing them with food.

Mut was identified with both Bast and Sekhmet and could assume the form of either a cat or lion—indeed she is more often associated with cats than she is with vultures.

She was probably the original god of Thebes and was Amun's wife when his cult became popular in the area.

Amun and Mut had no children of their own but they adopted first Montu and then later Khonsu, with whom they formed the Theban triad.

Neferten

Neferten was the son of Ptah and Sekhmet and the third member of the Memphis triad. His name means 'Atum the younger' and therefore he has links with Atum of Heliopolis. He represents the divine lotus and so was the god of fragrance. The form of water-lily known as the lotus can be observed to close its petals as darkness falls, then, turning to the east, to open them again to greet the rising sun. The plant was therefore closely associated with the sun and the solar gods. According to one myth the sun rose each morning out of a blue lotus.

The Greeks called Neferten Iphtimis and identified him with Prometheus, possibly as his father Ptah was said to be the discoverer of fire. He is usually seen in human form carrying a khepesh or curved sword. Upon his head he bears an open lotus flower, and at other times he follows his mother's example and has a lion's head. At Buto in the Delta he was considered to be the son of Uchet the cobra goddess, who at times also takes on a leonine form.

Neit

Neit, or Neeth as the Greeks called her (they equated her with their own Athena, goddess of war and wisdom), was the patron deity of the western Delta city of Sais, which in the seventh century BCE became the capital of all Egypt.

Neit's name may have its origin in a word meaning either 'that which is' or perhaps more likely 'the terrifying'. The former conforms to her role as creator, whilst the latter reflects her position as a goddess of war.

She is represented visually as a woman wearing the crown of Lower Egypt, which was known as 'net', suggesting the possibility that she was originally a personification of the crown itself. Her symbol was the bee, which throughout the ages has been associated with royalty and been a symbol of kingship.

In earliest times she was a goddess of hunting (as was Athena). This is represented in her personal emblems, which were two arrows crossing over a shield and a pair of bows in a single bowcase. In early forms of burial weapons or knives were placed around the coffin of the deceased, and this may have been associated with her cult.

The followers of Ra, the sun god,

believed Neit to be his mother. According to early myths she was the first of all the gods and after creating the world alone she became the virgin mother of the sun. She was the great mother goddess of the Egyptians. Myths describe how she emerged from the chaotic waters and formed the primeval mound to rest upon, then, raising her voice, uttered the words of power and created light and the first gods. Finally she gave birth to the sun, who rose as a child on the western horizon. As she was the first being in the universe to give birth, she was credited with inventing the act, and she presided over the births of mortals.

As a goddess of wisdom it was to her that the gods turned for advice, as in the trial of Set, when she acted as arbitrator. Like many other Egyptian deities her sacred animal was the cat.

Neit was especially popular in the Twenty-sixth Dynasty when Egypt enjoyed a time of stability and prosperity. In the beliefs associated with her we may observe a local goddess rising to national status and acquiring the attributes of the great and powerful goddess Nut.

She was one of the four goddesses to guard the bodies of the dead and the canopic jars, which were protected by the four sons of Horus. She was known as the patroness of weavers. Mummy wrappings and bandages were called the gift of Neit.

The Greek historian Plutarch recorded an inscription from Neit's temple at Sais, which read:

> I am all that has been, that is, and all that will be. No mortal has yet been able to lift the veil which covers me.

Nekhebet

Nekhebet was worshipped in the town of Nekheb in southern Egypt which has roots dating back some 8,000 years. The archaeological remains discovered there prove it to be one of Egypt's oldest settlements.

In the form of a vulture goddess, Nekhebet protected the kings of Upper Egypt, just as the goddess Edjo was the protectress of the monarchy of the Lower Kingdom.

Her iconography shows her wearing the white crown of Upper Egypt, with which she is associated. The king would wear this crown on state occasions with a representation of Nekhebet in the form of a vulture's head upon his brow, whilst his principal queen was provided with a head-dress modelled on the vulture. In jewellery and papyrus art she is shown with her wings outstretched in protection, often hovering above the pharaoh and holding in her claws the hieroglyphic symbol the 'shem', which means 'to encircle' and 'infinity', and represents lordship over all that the sun encircles.

Nekhebet was also considered to be a goddess of childbirth, looking after mothers and children, and may be seen in wall paintings suckling the royal child and sometimes even the king himself.

Nephthys

Nephthys, the daughter of Geb and Nut, was one of the Heliopolian Eniad, in which she was the wife and sister of Set. Her loyalty, however, seems to have been to Osiris and Isis, her brother and sister, rather than to her husband, for she helped Isis to collect the dismembered parts of Osiris which had been cast into the Nile by Set and together they embalmed his body. With Isis she mourned the death of Osiris and later she became the protectress of the dead along with Isis, Neit and Selket.

According to another myth she encouraged Osiris to drink a large quantity of wine and then seduced him, eventually giving birth to the god Anubis.

The Egyptian form of her name was Nebethoot or Nebthet and she wore the hieroglyph of her name upon her head. Like her sister Isis she is shown at times with winged arms and could take on the form of a kite.

Nun

Nun or Nu was the name that the Egyptians gave to the chaos which existed before form. This god was the personification of the primal waters, the dark liquid mass that contained the potential for all things.

The texts describe Nun as having no surface as he stretched into each direction further than the imagination could comprehend. From him came Ra the creator.

Following the creation of the universe Nun continued to exist both beyond the boundaries of the universe, within the waters of the earth and in the sacred lakes and in the Nile.

In religious art he is seen as a bearded man waist-high in water, often supporting above him the sacred solar barque, Manjet.

Osiris

The name Osiris was the Greek form of the Egyptian Usire, and the Greeks identified him with their own gods of the underworld, Dionysus and Hades.

Osiris is represented as a man wrapped in a mummy's bindings holding in his crossed arms the ceremonial crook and flail. Upon his head he wears the tall white crown of Upper Egypt. Often his skin is coloured green, which symbolized regeneration and growth.

In the beginning Osiris was a vegetation god governing the death and rebirth of the crops, but later he became associated with the death of man and so as a funerary deity he was one of the most revered and popular of all Egypt's gods.

When Osiris was born wonderful singing was heard in the heavens and a loud voice called out proclaiming, 'Now has come the lord of all things.' Tremendous was the rejoicing throughout the land, the hearts of the people were gladdened, and rumour spread along both banks of the Nile that a great and wise king had been born amongst them.

According to the Egyptian myths Osiris was once a king upon the earth, his rule following those of Ra his grandfather and Geb his father. Before the reign of Osiris the tribes of Egypt were nomadic hunters constantly at war with each other as they travelled up and down the Nile valley, but with his sister Isis as his queen, Osiris set about civilizing his people. First he taught them the arts of agriculture and instructed them in the manufacturing of agricultural tools and implements. He showed them how to grow crops of wheat and then how to grind it for baking bread. They then learned how to raise vines to make wine, and in areas unsuited for grape production Osiris taught them how to brew beer from barley.

Osiris also founded temples and had them decorated with fine carvings, statues and paintings. He formulated the rituals of worship and religious practices, encouraging his people to live noble and just lives, constructed towns and provided the citizens with just laws.

When he was satisfied that his kingdom was civilized and that his people led contented and meaningful lives, he went from Egypt, travelling abroad with Thoth, Anubis and Wapwawet to civilize the rest of the world. Behind him he left his queen Isis to rule in his place.

Set, Osiris's brother, was envious of the position and power of Isis and sought to take the throne for himself. Isis, however, was wise and strong and she quickly defeated his rebellion. As Set was the brother of both Isis and Osiris, he escaped punishment and was allowed to retain his freedom.

Osiris brought many lands under his rule, not by violence and the force of arms, but by gentleness and persuasion. His army marched to the sound of joyful songs and the playing of sweet music, not the chants of war and the clash of spears against shields.

Only after bringing the benefits of civilization to the whole of the earth did Osiris's mind turn to thoughts of home and returning to Egypt. Once back in Egypt, he found the land prosperous and peaceful under the wise and loving care of Isis. But after a time jealousy again surged in his brother's heart, and quietly and diligently Set planned his destruction. He formed an alliance with the queen of Ethiopia, and aided by 70 of her people, he waited for his chance.

Using secretly obtained measurements of the dimensions of the king's body, Set had a rich chest fashioned and ornamented with great skill and artistry. Such was its size and shape that it would only accommodate the king's body and no other. This task completed, Set held an elaborate feast in honour of Osiris's reign. Apart from Osiris the only other guests were his own confederates.

At the feast the chest was brought before the assembled company with great show and ceremony. It was greeted with cries of delight and shouts of admiration. Set, as if joking, promised that it should be a gift to whosoever it would fit, and offered Osiris the chance to be the first to try. Obligingly the unsuspecting god climbed into the box. As soon as he lay within its confines the conspirators seized their chance and slamming down the lid they nailed it firmly in place and sealed the cracks with molten lead. The wonderful chest had become a deadly coffin. With Osiris firmly entombed, Set had the chest carried to the mouth of the Nile and cast into the sea.

News of the fate of Osiris came to the ears of Isis and she immediately set out to find his body, for she knew the dead could not rest until they had received a proper burial with the correct rites and ceremonies. Long she searched, asking all that she met for news of her beloved husband, but none were able to help. Eventually her searching carried her to the point where the Nile meets the sea. There she saw children playing, and they told her that the chest had been cast adrift by Set.

Consulting oracles, Isis discovered further details of the whereabouts of her husband's body. The chest, she was told, had been washed ashore on the coast of Byblos in Phoenicia, and rested for a while amongst the branches of a tamorisk bush. Encouraged by the vitality of the god which it held, the bush grew rapidly, becoming a mighty tree and forming a solid trunk about the chest. The ruler of Byblos, King Melcarthus, and his queen saw the tree and were highly impressed. They had it cut down and from its trunk commanded that a pillar be made to support the roof of the royal palace. In this position it exuded such a sweat odour that its fame spread far and wide.

Isis left Egypt and travelled to Byblos. Once there she sat at a fountain that was situated outside the king's residence. There she remained, speaking to no one except the queen's own handmaidens. To these she was most helpful. She would braid their hair, tying it with great skill, and perfumed them with the sweet fragrance of her own breath. Returning to their mistress, they told her of their meeting

with the strange woman. The queen's curiosity was immediately aroused and she summoned Isis to the palace and was so impressed by her skills that she gave her the position of nurse to one of her young sons.

Dark rumours spread around the palace however of the strange practices of the new nurse. It was told that each night she would wait until all had retired. Once all was quiet, she would enter the great hall and build up the fire into a raging furnace. When the flames were at their highest she would plunge her charge, the prince, in amongst them, after which she would change herself into a swallow and fly around the great pillar singing sorrowfully as if in mourning for a lost loved one.

News of these alarming habits came to the notice of the queen, who, fearing for the safety of her child, set out to discover if the tales were true. Concealing herself in the great hall, she waited for night to fall. Then, just as she had been told, Isis came forth and after building up the fire, cast the child into the flames.

With a scream the queen sprang from her hiding place and pulled the child from the fire. Isis turned to her and chastised her severely, explaining that by her foolish and hasty action she had deprived her son of eternal life.

Isis went on to explain her true identity to the astonished queen and revealed the events that had led to her coming to Byblos. Finally she begged that she might be given the pillar that supported the roof of the palace.

When the king heard of the goddess's presence he did all that he could to make her welcome and was quick to grant her request. The pillar was carefully removed and the chest cut out from its heart. Isis had the chest carried aboard a ship and sailed back to Egypt, accompanied by Maneros, the king's eldest son, while the remains of the tree that she left behind were anointed with myrrh and worshipped and venerated by the Byblians as a holy relic.

During the voyage Isis found that she could no longer keep from opening the coffin, so, raising the lid, she gazed lovingly upon Osiris's cold face and kissed his still lips, tears falling upon him from her eyes. Wondering what great secret the chest contained, Maneros came up behind her, but when she heard him she turned around in anger and the brightness of her tear-reddened eyes burnt his flesh and caused him to fall dead on the deck.

In the meantime, as Isis had been searching for the body of Osiris, Set had taken the vacant throne of Egypt. Under his rule the supporters of Osiris were persecuted and injustice prevailed. When Isis returned to the land of Egypt Set's followers hunted her as a fugitive, driving her to seek refuge in the dark swamps of the Delta, but Ra, her grandfather, saw her plight from his seat in the heavens and sent Anubis to be her guide.

Isis hid the body of Osiris from the eyes of Set. However whilst he was out hunting one night by moonlight he chanced upon her chosen hiding-place. Recognizing the chest, he opened it and had the body of Osiris removed and cut into 14 pieces, which were cast into the Nile in the belief that crocodiles would devour them and thus deny Osiris eternal life. But because of their love for Osiris and their fear of the wrath of Isis the crocodiles did not eat the flesh of the god, and the pieces were carried by the waters of the Nile and cast upon the banks, all that is except the phallus, which was consumed by a fish of the species Oxyrhychid.

When Isis discovered Set's evil deed she was filled with greater sorrow then before. Accompanied by her sister Nephthys she sailed down the Nile searching out the scattered parts of Osiris's body.

According to one version of the story as she found each piece she buried it, and upon the spot was raised a temple to his name, thus explaining the proliferation of his temples.

A second version of the story tells that the gods Anubis and Thoth descended from heaven to assist Isis and Nephthys. Together they took the separate parts of the body and made Osiris whole again, then wrapped him in the bandages of a mummy. Isis took the form of a kite and used her wings to blow air into his nostrils, restoring his soul to life and making it free to depart into the otherworld. Still in the form of a bird, she came to rest on the body of her dead husband and using her magic she conceived their son Horus.

For many years Set reigned and Isis remained in hiding with her son. In time Horus grew strong and well practised in the arts of combat, waiting for the day when he would be strong enough to avenge his father's slayer.

Among the swamps of the Delta Horus raised an army comprised of the faithful followers of his father and those who hated Set for his wrongdoing. The angry hawk of the sun glared down from their banners of war. Then, following a sign from his father which was revealed to him in a dream, Horus called his army to his side and marched to battle.

Set assembled his forces and drew them up in lines of battle upon the fields of Edfu. His army was strong, but that of Horus was increased when many of Set's own warriors, still faithful to Osiris and Isis,

broke from the ranks and joined Horus. Following a bitter and bloody struggle, Horus won the field. Set was driven forth in disarray, and the victors pursued him up to the eastern borders of Egypt. Finally he sought to make a stand at Zaru. Gathering the remnants of his force, he prepared to meet the army of Horus once again.

The fighting at Zaru was fierce, the killing lasted many days, and the mounds of the dead grew high with broken bodies. Beneath the circling vultures Horus and Set fought with all their might, both suffering many wounds, and when for a brief moment the two stood face to face the sound of their cries of rage shook the earth and caused those around them to quake with fear. The gods engaged each other with the fury of wild beasts, cutting and slashing, heedless to pain. Set was driven back as the superior strength of Horus began to show, and taking advantage of a moment's respite he escaped to the ranks of his supporters. But for all his powers, the hawk god had lost an eye to the hand of Set.

Eventually Set was overcome, and the last defeated and bloody remains of his once proud army fled across the border and out of Egypt. Thoth came down from heaven and healed the wounds of both combatants. Then Set was summoned to appear before a council of gods to answer for his crimes. They passed judgement that Horus was the rightful king of Egypt and he became a well-loved ruler, just as his father had been before him.

Eventually as time passed Horus too became tired of earthly kingship and handed his throne to a human successor. From then on the rule of the gods upon earth was ended. Thereafter kings took the name 'Horus' throughout their lives and after death they took the name 'Osiris'. Indeed when a king died his heir would add authority to his claim to the throne by assuming the title of Horus and presiding over the burial of the deceased Osiris. This practice was followed when succession was direct from father to son but could also be used to legitimatize the ascendance to the throne of those not of royal descent, for example when Tutankhamun died without male offspring he was followed by his uncle Ay, who although not of royal blood, assumed the title of Horus and conducted the rituals of burial for his nephew, therefore validating his claim to the throne.

Pakhet

Pakhet, whose name means 'she who scratches', was the local lion goddess of the Middle Kingdom necropolis in the Oryx Nome of Upper Egypt.

During the Eighteenth Dynasty King Hatshepsut had carved from the rock a cavernous temple which he dedicated to Pakhet. The Greeks identified her with Artemis and named the temple Spios Artemidos, 'the cave of Artemis'.

Ptah

Ptah, his wife Sekhmet and his son Neferten formed the Memphite Triad. Ptah was associated with Hephaestus by the Greeks, and as he was the god of blacksmiths the Romans called him Vulcan after their own god of the forge. He was an earth god and had links with the underworld. Visually he was represented as a human wrapped in the bindings of a mummy. In his hands, which remained free of the bandages, he held the waas sceptre, the djed and the ankh, symbolizing domination, stability and life. As alternatives to these he is sometimes seen holding the crook and flail, and resembles images of Osiris, with whom he shared many attributes.

At Memphis he was believed to be the original creator god, pre-existing Nun the primal chaos. By a prolonged effort of meditation and pouring out of love, he brought Nun into existence together with Nunet, his female counterpart. Nun and Nunet in turn gave birth to Atum who was given the title 'the thought of Ptah', the Egyptians considering him to represent the heart of Ptah, and the heart being the seat of the mind. Finally Thoth came into being and was called 'Ptah's tongue', for it was through Thoth that all things received their name.

By the Twentieth Dynasty Ptah ranked third of the gods, standing behind only Ra and Amun. He was believed to have invented the methods and techniques of the craftsman and was the god of masons. His high priest held the title 'master builder'.

To the south of his great temple at Memphis a bull was kept, named Hap, or Apis, to give him his more common Greek name. This animal was considered to be the physical manifestation of Ptah. The bull was provided with a harem of cows, his needs were carefully attended to and he would often attain a great age.

The Apis bull was always chosen for his special markings: he had a black coat with white spots on his back and a white triangle upon the forehead. When the bull died, the priest of Ptah would scour the length of Egypt looking for a calf with the correct markings. When found, he would be installed as the new Apis amid great rejoicing and ceremony. The calf's mother also received special attention, being well cared for throughout her life, and at death her body was mummified.

Within the temple complex stood a building devoted to the embalming of the dead Apis bulls. Following mummification the body would be deposited in a special crypt reserved for the bulls in the necropolis. These crypts were of impressive proportions. An early tomb devoted to Apis consists of a gallery over 68 metres long, whilst a later example constructed in the Twenty-sixth Dynasty exceeds 198 metres in length.

Ra

Ra was the great solar god of Heliopolis, city of the sun. The word ra probably meant 'creator', and it was first applied to the sun. Only later did it become the name of the god.

Ra had many forms and many names. Perhaps the most important of these was Ra-Harrakte, who was shown in Egyptian art as a falcon-headed god wearing the solar disc and the uraeus, a rearing cobra with inflated hood worn on the brow of a ruler. Harrakte was a particular manifestation of Horus, that of 'Horus of the horizon', the birthplace of the sun. It was in the guise of Ra-Harrakte that the sun god was worshipped at Heliopolis.

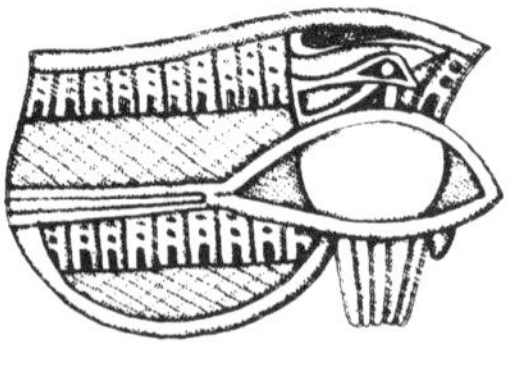

Heliopolis was Ra's main cult centre. It was here, his priests declared, that he had first become manifest. Visitors were shown the precise spot where he entered into existence and it was here that the primal hill had stood, having risen from the chaos of Nun. The position of the hill was commemorated by the erection of a huge obelisk. In time the obelisk, known as the Benben Stone, also symbolized the life-giving rays of the sun, and became an object of worship in its own right.

According to Heliopolian myth Ra was originally named Atum. At first he lay

silent within Nun, wrapped in the bud of a lotus. With his eyes and mouth firmly closed he held his bright flame of solar light safe from the crushing power of chaos. Eventually tiring of his inactivity, he climbed from the darkness and revealed himself in all his burning glory, and he was no longer Atum: he had become Ra.

Then he formed the first pair of gods, Shu and his sister Tefnut. They gave birth to the twin gods Geb and Nut, who were in turn the parents of Osiris, Isis, Set and Nephthys. Ra and the eight gods formed the Ogdoad and were worshipped together at Heliopolis.

Although Ra fathered the gods Shu and Tefnut, he did not himself have a partner until much later when he was given a wife, Rat, whose name was a feminine form of Ra. Rat also had other names such as Iusas, Eusos and Uert Hekeu, meaning 'great of magic'.

Following the Heliopolian Ogdoad came the other gods and later mankind, all born from the sweat and tears of Ra.

The universe Ra created for his children to live in was far different from the present world. It was known as the 'First Time' and was an age when the gods and men walked side by side upon the earth. Ra himself was the first king of the earth, ruling from Heliopolis with Ma'at his daughter, the personification of truth and justice, by his side. Each day it was said Ra would rise after his morning meal and board his sacred boat. With his scribe he would travel over the 12 divisions of his kingdom, spending one twelfth of the daylight hours in each of them.

After a time Ra became weary of his life on earth and longed to leave the responsibility to another. So Nut assumed the form of a cow and, mounting her back,

he was raised up into the heavens. With the sun god's departure, Thoth the moon god took his place and ruled over the earth.

From that time onwards each morning Ra would appear in the east above Manu, 'the mountains of the sunrise', and traverse the sky in the Manjet boat, 'the barque of millions of years'. The crew of the Manjet boat was made up of the gods of creation, wisdom and magic. Horus stood at the helm, whilst Thoth was positioned at the bow, destroying Ra's enemies as they progressed. Ra wore the double crown of the united Egypt with the uraeus, spitting flames before him.

Deep in the waters of Nun there lived the greatest of Ra's enemies, Apep or Apophis, a gigantic serpent. As the golden barque sailed overhead the serpent would rise up, attempting to destroy the god, only to be cast down again into the abyss, defeated by power of the gods. The battle between the gods and Apep was unceasing. During a solar eclipse, however, the Egyptians believed that the barque had been consumed. Storms that obscured the sun also provided evidence that Apep had been successful, if only temporarily.

According to other myths Ra was born with each dawn and was destined to die at sunset. His age increased through the day. In the morning he was a child, at noon he attained the full strength of manhood, but as the afternoon passed into evening he would age and eventually die with the approach of darkness.

Through the night Ra assumed a ram's head and took the name Auf, meaning 'flesh' or 'corpse' and travelled upon the Meseket boat or 'the night barque'. During the 12 hours of darkness Upuqut the opener of roads stood at the prow.

Other myths tell that the stars made up

the crews of the sacred barques. 'Those who can never set', i.e. the stars which although present in the daytime sky cannot be observed due to the sun's brightness, manned the day barque, while 'those who can never become weary', that is the stars which are observed for only a short period each night, are said to have gone one by one to the west to crew the night barque.

Through the 12 hours of darkness Ra again visited his 12 provinces but now each was peopled by terrifying snakes and monstrous demons, each threatening to ensnare the boat and arrest its progress.

Ra was recognized throughout the whole of Egypt as the creator of the universe and all the gods became identified with him. In the Old Kingdom the pharaohs claimed to be the sons of Ra and wore the eye and the uraeus as symbols of divine authority.

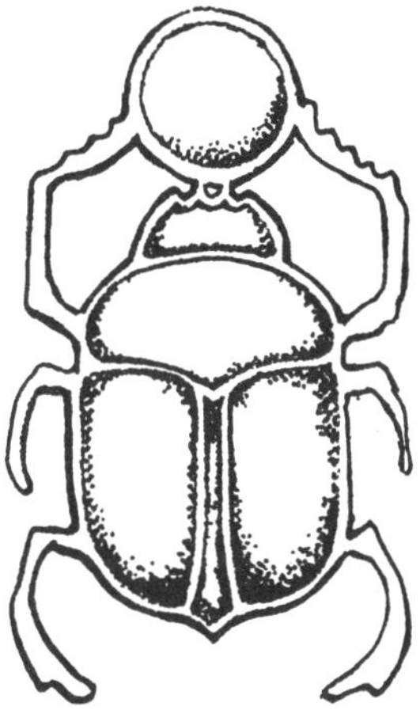

Sebek

Sebek, called Suchos by the Greeks, was a crocodile god much favoured by the kings of the Twelfth and Thirteenth Dynasties. Many of the rulers of this period chose to bear names such as Sebekhotep, which means 'Sebek is satisfied'.

According to the pyramid texts Sebek was the son of Neit, goddess of warfare and later protector of the dead. His main place of worship was in the Nome of Faiyum of which he was the patron deity. His temple lay in this Nome at the town of Shedet, which the Greeks called Crocodilopolis. Within the temple there was a holy lake where a sacred crocodile was kept named Petsuchos, 'he who belongs to Suchos (Sebek)'.

He was also worshipped at Kom Ombo, where he replaced Set in a triad of gods, becoming the husband of Hathor and the father of Khonsu. Whether he was considered to be the brother of Osiris and Isis is not known.

In Egyptian art Sebek is represented as either a crocodile or a man with a crocodile's head. He was a god of water and it was believed that the Nile issued from his throne. But he also had associations with the gods Ra and Horus as solar gods and was linked with the creation myths. Perhaps this was because the Egyptian could observe the crocodile climbing out of the Nile, as the creator had done from the dark waters of Nun, and producing eggs upon the land, again repeating the act of the creator gods.

Sekhmet

The name Sekhmet is derived from the Greek Sakhmis and meant 'the powerful' or 'the mightiest'. Sekhmet was the feared goddess of war and was represented in sacred art as a lioness or a woman with a lioness's head. She was the daughter of Ra, and one of her commonest titles was Nesert, meaning 'flame', which emphasized this link. (Uatchet, the protectress of Ra and the kings, was also called the lady of the flame.)

Sekhmet was married to the god Ptah and as such was a member of the Memphis triad. Their son was Neferten, the lotus god, although some myths say that he was the child of Bast rather than Sekhmet. In later times Sekhmet and Bast were the watchers and guardians of the east and west, as Nekhebet and Wadjet were of the south and north, and so Sekhmet was also known as the lady of the mountains of the setting sun.

A second goddess with which Sekhmet was associated is Hathor, and in the story Ra and his rebellious subjects the two are interchangeable—some versions say Hathor, others Sekhmet. There is a temple to Sekhmet-Hathor in the western Delta and in the temple of Abydos, Hathor is given the title 'mistress of the mansion of

Sekhmet'. Another of Sekhmet's many titles is 'the lady of the bright red linen', which may refer to the colour of the earth in her homeland—or perhaps more likely to the blood-splattered garments of her enemies.

When the king rode into battle at the head of his troops it was Sekhmet who stood in the chariot by his side, encouraging victory and protecting him from harm. She was deeply feared by her enemies and even the demons of Set and the serpent Apophis fell before her. The burning winds that blew from the desert was her breath and the Egyptians believed that a fiery aura surrounded her body.

Plague and pestilence were also her doing and so appeals to her could bring about relief. This later developed into the belief that she was a healer, and she would be called upon by the doctors to assist them in their work. Her priests would accompany the physicians and while they worked would recite prayers to heal the sick. In later times they practised medicine themselves.

When the royal quarters were moved to Thebes, the local goddess Ma'at, the consort of Thoth, became merged with Sekhmet. As Thoth was considered by some to be a particular aspect of Ptah, so Ma'at became a part of Sekhmet. In her temple Amenhotep III had almost 600 statues raised in her honour.

Sekhmet's head-dress, the solar disc surrounded by the uraeus, suggests the astrological symbol of Leo the lion and the sign's ruling planet is the sun.

Set

Set is perhaps one of the oldest of all the Egyptian gods, and also one of the most complex. Originally the god of the Lower Kingdom he became associated with foreign peoples, possibly because they worshipped similar gods with whom he could be identified. Then, as aliens were so often mistrusted by the conservative natives of Egypt, he became the enemy of the gods.

His worship was known in the earliest predynastic times when his cult centre was at Nebet on the bank of the Nile, north of Luxor. The town was situated on one of the main routes in and out of Egypt and was on the supply road to the gold mines of the desert. Nebet actually means 'gold town' and one of Set's names is Nebty, 'he of the gold town'. He was also a god of thunder.

Set was represented in carvings by a strange composite beast. The body was like that of a greyhound, he had a long forked tail standing stiffly upright, his face had a curved and extended snout or nose, and his ears were pricked up but with sharply flattened tips. His flesh was deathly white and his hair was red. In dynastic times there are illustrations of Set with a dagger driven into his head, showing that by this time he was seen as harmful to humankind

and a source of danger which must be ritually countered. Each month it was believed that he attacked and consumed the moon, causing its disappearance from the night-time sky.

According to legend, the earth god Geb divided the earth into two parts, giving the northern part, or Lower Egypt, to Set's brother Horus, and the south, or Upper Egypt, to Set. Each god ruled justly over his people. With the unification of Egypt, Horus of the north and Set of the south were shown together facing each other with the symbol of unity between them. However this equality between the two gods appears to have lapsed into a state of polarity. There *were* kings, such as Sekhemib during the Second Dynasty, who preferred the god Set, but overall Horus was the foremost of the two.

The two gods moved further and further apart as their relationship transformed. First Horus became the dominant partner then the eclipsed Set became his adversary. Originally united, the two gods became opposed as Set became the mortal enemy of Horus.

About the year 1670 BCE invaders began to infiltrate the eastern Delta from lands to the East. Known as the Hyksos people, they gained the throne of Egypt in the Fifteenth and Sixteenth Dynasties, enjoying their position for over 400 years. They identified Set with their own god of war Baal, and worshipped him under the name of Sutekh.

In the Memphite pantheon Set was the brother of Osiris, Isis and Nephthys, the latter goddess being also his wife. The Hyskos, however, gave him two wives of their own pantheon, Anath and Astarte. (Astarte was a goddess of war comparable to Sekhmet and is sometimes shown in carvings as being lion-headed, while at others she appears riding naked in her battle chariot.) These two goddesses were accepted and worshipped by the Egyptians as wives of Set even after the eventual departure of the Hyksos, when Set's statues were destroyed and his name forbidden to be recorded or voiced.

Besides being a god of foreigners Set also became a god of the desert. He assumed the name 'the red god', representing the deeply inhospitable desert to the east. His name was linked to evil and malevolence, and all manner of dangerous animals were associated with him and his cult. Red-coated animals were his accomplices and even men with red hair were held in suspicion. The Greeks identified him with their Typhon. In legend he was reported to have entered the world by bursting violently through the side of Nut, his mother.

Ramesses, the founder of the Twenty-first Dynasty came from a family of the eastern Delta that appears to have held a special relationship with Set, and indeed he named his son Seti I in the god's honour.

Sokar

Long before the city of Memphis was built there was a sizable necropolis on the site, where the people of the area gathered to bury their dead, and in the earliest predynastic times the god Sokar appears to have been worshipped as the protector of this place, originally in the form of a simple fetish. Later he became identified with the peregrine falcon, a bird often observed flying high above the desert's edge where the necropolis was situated, and finally in the Old Kingdom he was represented in human form with the head of a hawk.

Sokar was usually shown seated upon a stone or a throne, holding the symbols of power and kingship, the waas sceptre and the ankh. His appearance changed until by the time of the New Kingdom some thousand years later he was represented as a hawk-headed mummy, thus emphasizing his funerary connections. He wore upon his hawk head a complex crown consisting of the Atef crown, a solar disc, two horns and two cobras.

His great annual celebration took place on the twenty-sixth day of the fourth month of the season of Akhet. This was on the eve of the winter's sowing. The rituals performed at this time strongly imply that Sokar had origins as an agricultural deity, as did Osiris, Egypt's main god of the underworld. His image was pulled across the then barren fields in a barque mounted upon a sledge, and in this way he blessed the earth and ensured both the land's fertility and the prosperity of his followers.

After the city of Memphis was built the god Ptah became its principal god, but Sokar was given the position of his aid and funerary god. The patron of goldsmiths and the guardian of the door to the underworld, he was also believed to be the manufacturer of the bones of the king and was responsible for the mixing of sacred aromatic oils and resins to produce the unguents and incenses required in the ceremonies and rituals of the gods.

He was believed to live in a secret cavern named Imhet, deep in the underworld, and his main shrine, the Shetayet, was in Memphis, close to the temple of Ptah. Although it is well described in ancient writings it has never been discovered.

Gradually the two gods Ptah and Sokar became fused into a single deity under the name of Ptah-Sokar, and eventually they were both to become a part of the god Osiris.

Tefnut and Shu

The first beings created by Ra were the twins Tefnut and Shu. The name Shu means literally 'to raise', for it is he who holds aloft the sky. It was also said that he held apart his two children, Geb the earth god and Nut the sky goddess. He was therefore the god of air, and was also considered to be the god of light.

In sacred art Shu is shown in human form with an ostrich feather on his head, the ostrich feather being the hieroglyph of his name. Another of his symbols was a representation of the four pillars which stood at the four corners of the earth and aided him in his task of holding up the sky.

While the priests of Hermopolis claimed that Horus followed Ra as king of Egypt, at Heliopolis it was believed that Shu was Ra's successor. He later abdicated in favour of his son Geb. His farewell party is reputed to have been a noisy affair which lasted the whole of nine days.

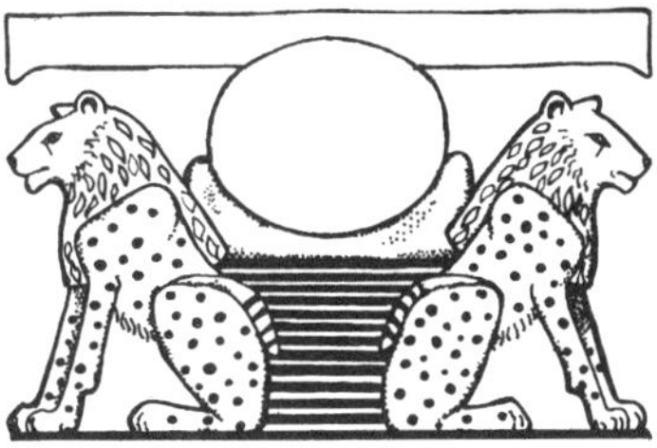

Tefnut was Shu's twin sister and wife. She was the goddess of moisture, and helped her husband in supporting the sky. The Greeks identified her with Artemis and in sacred art she is shown as either a lioness or a woman with a lion's head.

At Nay-ta-hut, which the Greeks named Leontopolis, 'the city of the lions', she was worshipped as a lion, and it was in the form of lions that Tefnut and Shu guarded the eastern and western horizons. Lions were also carved upon beds to protect the sleeper through the night.

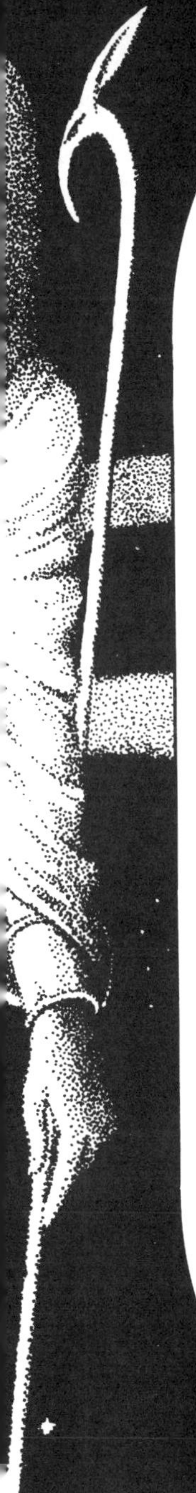

Thoth

Originally named either Djehuti or Zehuti by the Egyptians, Thoth was given his better-known name by the Greeks. They linked him with their own god Hermes, and like Hermes he was considered to be the god of wisdom, writing and invention. He was also the messenger and spokesman of the gods and finally a lunar god.

Worship of Thoth dates from at least the pre-dynastic period, as his standard appears on artifacts of this time, and his name Djehuti may indicate that he originated in the Nome of Dehut in Lower Egypt.

He is represented as a man with the head of an ibis, which is often crowned by the crescent moon. The baboon is also sacred to him, for in Hermopolis he merged with the local baboon god Hedj-Wer.

According to the priests of Hermopolis it

was Thoth in the form of an ibis who hatched (by the power of his voice alone), the world egg from which all creation issued.

Other myths relate that in the chaos of Nun he awoke from aeons of slumber and, opening his mouth, issued the first sound. This original sound assumed form and became the first eight beings, four gods and four goddesses, the Ogdoad. The Ogdoad represented the elemental forces that existed before the creation. They formed four pairs, the male of each pair being frog-headed and the female serpent-headed. The names of these deities, male and female respectively, were Nun and Nunet, representing the primeval waters, Theh and Hehet, infinite space and eternity, Kek and Keket, darkness, and Amun and Amunet, invisibility. At Khemenu, Thoth's main cult centre, they were regarded as the oldest of all the gods, for it was said that they created the sun and all that followed.

The pyramid texts link the name of Thoth to the family tree of Osiris, but usually he is seen as an independent deity, employed by Osiris as vizier and scribe, functions which he was later to perform in the service of Horus.

Another legend suggests that Thoth was the child of Horus and Set. It tells of Horus impregnating Set by tricking him into swallowing his seed hidden in a lettuce. As a result Thoth emerged from Set's forehead, although in a second version, of the late period, the seed appears upon Set's brow as a golden disc.

Thoth invented the arts and sciences, music and magic, and was the god of learning, but above all he was famed for being the creator of hieroglyphs, and was known as 'the lord of holy words'. Hieroglyphs themselves were known as 'the words of the gods'.

In early dynastic times the main cult centre of Thoth was in the town of Khemenu, the 'town of eight', and in even earlier times several gods were worshipped here. They were a hare goddess, a baboon god and the four frog gods and four serpent goddesses. It was the reptile gods who gave the place its name. The hare goddess, Wenet, gave her name to the Nome in which Khemenu was situated, and she was at times regarded as a demon. In European folklore the hare is associated with both the

moon and witchcraft, being next to the cat the most common animal of witches, either as a familiar or as a form assumed by the witch. The frog likewise has had similar associations throughout history, whilst the links between serpents and magic are many. When Thoth adopted the baboon, already associated with the moon, it came to represent his spirit.

To the west of Khemenu, or Hermopolis as the Greeks named it, lies the necropolis of the city. Here extensive underground passageways have been discovered. Given the name the Iberieum, they contain the bodies of thousands of mummified ibises and baboons. Close to the necropolis was a large artificial lake manually supplied with water and planted with trees and vegetation to provide an attractive habitat for the sacred ibises. A second burial place of ibises and baboons has been found at Saqqara, but it contains such a vast quantity of animals that its full extent has still to be determined.

Amongst the Egyptian magicians Thoth was called 'the elder' and his followers claimed access to his library of magical books. Here they spent their time deciphering the pages and learning the secret formulae that held the power to control all the forces of nature, even how to command the obedience of the gods themselves. Such was the magical knowledge of Thoth that his disciples named him 'Thoth three times very very greatest', which the Greeks translated as Hermes Trismegistus. Down the ages many magical texts and grimoires, in the main dating from the medieval period, have been spuriously attributed to Hermes Trismegistus.

After Horus stepped down from his earthly throne, his vizier Thoth took over and reigned, according to Hermopolis legend, for a period of 3,226 years, presiding over a peaceful and prosperous land. Then, like Osiris and Horus before him, he ascended to the place of the gods.

As god of men Thoth was the master of time. It was he who first divided the year into months of equal length consisting of 30 days each and added a further five intercalary days to make 365. According to one myth the goddess Nut gave birth to the sun, the stars and the planets. This so angered her father that he forbade her to have any further children in any month of the year. She went to Thoth and in a game of chance won from him five days which belonged to no month. On these five extra days she gave birth to the gods Osiris, Isis, Set, Nephthys and Horus.

The female counterpart of Thoth was the goddess Seshat. In temple paintings she is shown dressed in a leopard skin with an emblem upon her head in the form of a seven-pointed star, above which is a pair of inverted cow's horns suggesting a crescent moon.

She was not worshipped by the people of Egypt but was a personal god of the king, reserved for him alone. She aided and assisted the king in many ways: it was she who recorded the time allotted to him by the gods for his stay on earth, and from the Second Dynasty onwards, she helped him in the ritualized laying of the foundations of temples and the ceremony known as the stretching of the cord (referring to the mason's line used to measure out the limits of the building). Another aspect of the goddess is revealed by her title 'the foremost of libraries', clearly implying that she watched over her husband's many books.

Wadjet

Wadjet, also known by the name Edjo, was worshipped in predynastic times in the form of a cobra, sometimes winged. She was also known as Buto, named after the town in the northwest Delta which may have been the place of origin for her cult.

As the fire-spitting cobra Wadget she represented the eye of Ra, upon whose forehead she was stationed to protect him from his enemies. Also in a protective role, it was Wadjet who watched over Isis and the young Horus in their time in the swamps of the Delta, defending them from the raging Set.

She was the patron goddess of northern Egypt, the counterpart of Nekhebet, the vulture-headed goddess of Upper Egypt, and is shown as a snake wearing the red crown of Lower Egypt. The kings of the united land wore upon their brows figures of both the cobra (known in this form as the uraeus) and the vulture side by side. Together the two goddesses Wadjet and Nekhebet were known as Nebti, meaning 'the two mistresses'.

Wadjet was the royal cobra, and the other cobra goddesses, Renutet and Mertseger, were worshipped by the lower ranks in society. Renutet was a fertility deity, the goddess of harvests and childbirth. At times she appears with the solar disc upon her head. Mertseger was portrayed as a woman but could have the head of either a snake or a vulture. She was the guardian of the necropolis of Thebes. Wadjet can also appear as a lioness and sometimes, perhaps because of her association with Nekhebet, she, like Mertseger, takes the form of a vulture.

One of her names means 'the papyrus-coloured one' referring to the green colour of her skin, and according to the pyramid texts she created the papyrus swamps of the Delta in which she lived and was worshipped.

Animals

At some time or other practically all the animals of Egypt appear to have had links with the gods, and it is likely that many of the gods had their origin in the animal totems of the earliest predynastic period. This may be observed in the multitude of animal-headed gods and goddesses which existed later in the dynastic period.

Some animals became intermediaries between gods and men, and were offered gifts in exchange for securing favours from a particular god. Such events occurred in Memphis, where offerings were presented to the sacred bull Apis, the earthly representative of the solar god Ptah. Some came to symbolize the powerful forces of nature, others were the agents and accomplices of demons. Such would be thought, for instance, of a poisonous serpent who lived in a commonly visited place waiting to strike at the unwary.

Alternatively an animal may have become associated with a particular deity because it exhibited some special trait which linked the two. In this way the ibis with its curved beak resembling the crescent of the moon became the symbol of the lunar god Thoth.

Often animals sacred to a particular god were kept within the god's temple, either as a single animal or as a group. They were looked after with reverent care by the priests. Examples of this were the baboons and ibises kept at the temple of Thoth at Hermopolis, and the sacred cats of Isis which were carefully tended at Philae.

Ass

The ass was the traditional beast of burden and in Egyptian religion became an opponent of the sun god. It was told that 77 asses barred the way of the sun, seeking to prevent its rising at dawn. The ass symbolized Set, the great opponent of Osiris and Horus, and in Busiris loaves of bread stamped with images of an ass were given as symbolic offerings to the corn god Osiris.

Bennu Bird

Whilst the bennu bird is totally mythical, never having had a physical existence, it was considered to be a reality by the Egyptians. Usually represented in the form of a lapwing or heron-like bird, because of its connections with the cults of Ra and Osiris, its name was linked to that of the phoenix.

Bull

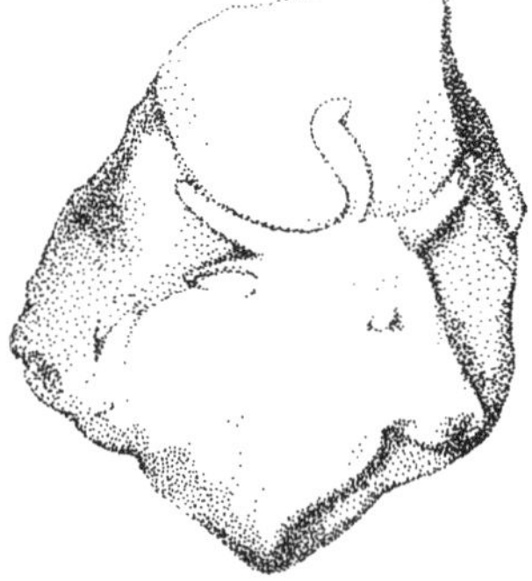

Bulls were associated with various gods throughout Egyptian history, as they were strong, vigorous beasts representing power and fertility.

The bull known as Buchis, for example, was kept by the priesthood of Hermonthis as the earthly incarnation of Ra and Osiris. It also embodied the soul of Mont. Sacred to the sun, the four-horned bull of Ra was believed to guard the roads of heaven and the hair of its coat was thought to change colour with each passing hour, while through the bull Mnevis worshippers and priests could converse with the god Atum-Ra at Heliopolis.

Because of the bull's powerful symbology the kings of the New Kingdom bore titles such as 'mighty bull' and 'strong bull of Horus'. In the art of the archaic period the ruler was often represented by an image of a bull. The god Nun wore a bull's head and one of the names given to the inundation of the Nile was 'the gift of the bull'. Skulls of bulls were used to decorate temples and altars and were a means of protecting a place from evil.

Cat

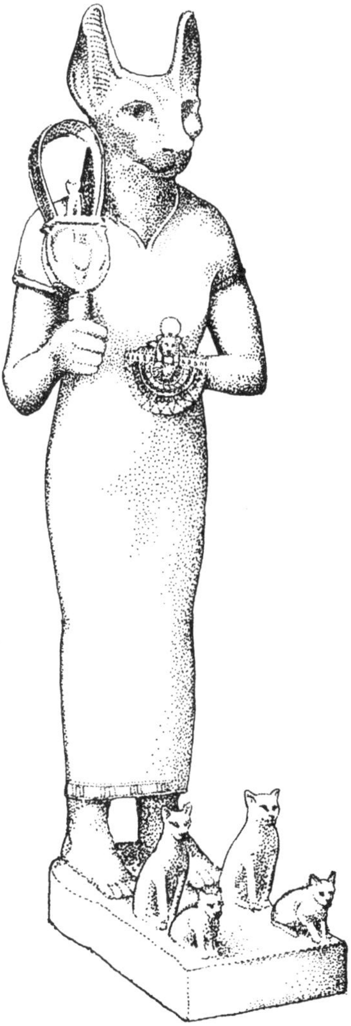

The cat was associated with the sun gods as the image of a scarab, the symbol of the sun god Khonsu, could be seen upon its head. Cats also caught and killed snakes, so in a land where poisonous snakes were a constant threat and source of danger they were obviously prized. There was also a myth in which the god Ra took the form of a cat to defeat the serpent Apophis.

By the time of the New Kingdom, the male cat was considered to be the incarnation of Ra, whilst the female cat was the eye of Ra, a title also given to the lion-headed goddess Sekhmet.

The cat was also sacred to Isis and was held in great respect by the ancient Egyptians. Killing a cat, whether by accident or design, was punishable by death. It is recorded that when a female cat reached maturity a mate would be found for her. He was carefully and specially selected with regard to size, colouring and temperament. When a cat died the members of the household shaved their eyebrows as a mark of mourning, and one ancient text tells that if a house should catch fire then the occupants would secure the safety of the household cats before attempting to extinguish the fire or save any of their possessions. Also in this text a belief is expressed that cats will deliberately seek to enter a burning building, perhaps stemming from the idea that the cat is the sacred creature of the sun god.

Cow

Cows in general were associated with the moon and were sacred to Isis because of her links with Hathor.

The Zenet cows were sacred to Hathor and were kept at her temple at Dendera. Hathor herself was worshipped in the form of a cow, and was shown in wall paintings either as a cow, or with a full cow's head or with merely its ears.

The Heset cow was believed at different times to be the mother of both the god Anubis and the Apis bull.

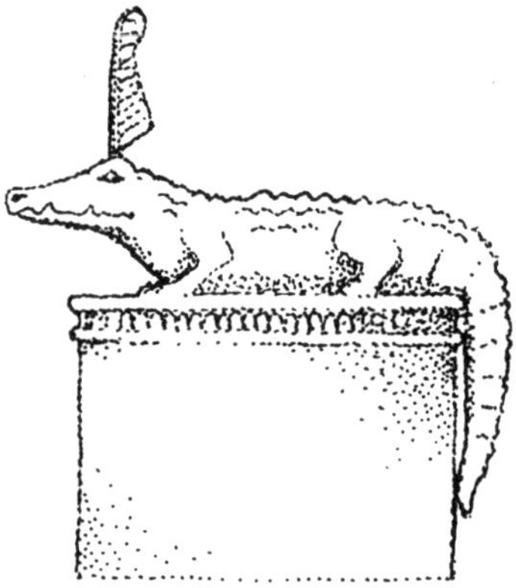

Crocodile

The dangerous Nile crocodiles were generally thought of as the allies of Set, and during the feast of Horus at Edfu images of crocodiles were cursed and destroyed. In other places however, temples were constructed to the beneficent crocodile gods such as those of Suchos at the Faiyum and Thebes. Here a crocodile named Petesuchos, 'he who belongs to Suchos', was kept. He wore gold rings in his ears and bangles on his legs, and lived in a sacred enclosure containing pools and shady plants for his comfort.

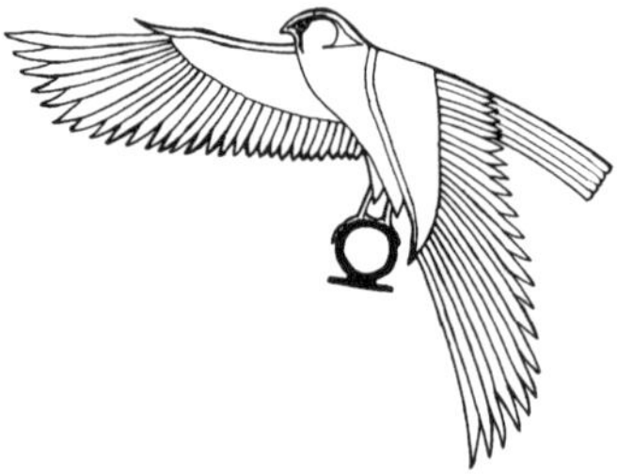

Falcon

The falcon was seen as the king of the birds as the lion was king of the animals, and like the lion it became a symbol of divine kingship. By the Fourth Dynasty the hieroglyph of a falcon represented the word for god.

The falcon was associated with various gods from the sun gods Ra and Horus to Mounth the warrior god and Sokar of the necropolis.

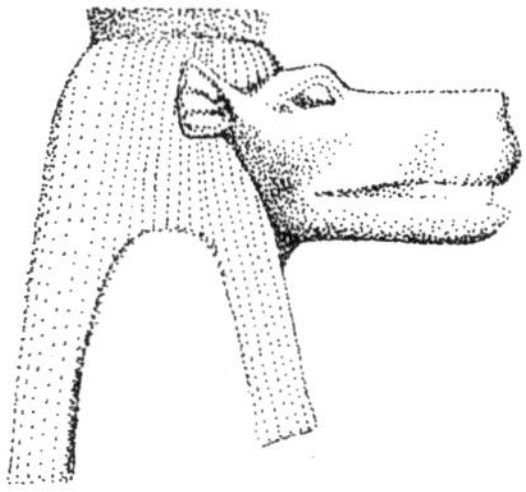

Hippopotamus

The hippopotamus held various associations: it was both a symbol of female fertility and a creature of Set. In the temple of Edfu the king, having ceremoniously assumed the identity of Horus, is depicted killing Set in the form of a white hippopotamus.

Ibis

The ibis was sacred to the god Thoth, and many lived at his temple at Hermopolis. Predominantly white with black areas upon its head, neck and wing tips, it may be seen accompanying Thoth in wall paintings throughout Egypt. Thousands of mummified ibises have been discovered at Hermopolis, Saqqara and elsewhere, emphasizing the reverence in which it was held.

Ichneumon

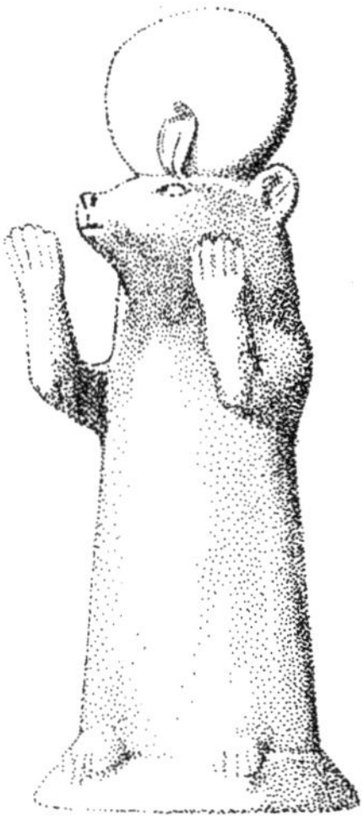

The ichneumon, the Egyptian mongoose or 'pharaoh's cat' as it is sometimes known, was both a representative of the sun god Horus and the underworld. Models of the animal with solar discs upon their heads were offered as gifts to the gods, and there are times when it was confused with the cat as the form taken by Ra when he fought with the serpent Apophis.

The ichneumon was especially prized by the Egyptians as it was a natural destroyer of crocodile eggs.

Lion

The lion was the animal of the sun, so in the lion the Egyptians saw the physical manifestation of the sun god Ra. Horus as the morning sun was depicted as lion-headed.

The sun could be both destructive and life-giving. In the former aspect the lion was associated with war and death as in the goddess Sekhmet, who like Horus was also known as the eye of Ra, whilst in the latter it symbolized protection and rebirth. The beds of the living and the biers upon which the mummified body rested were made in the form of lions or had legs and feet styled upon those of a lion.

The lion guarded temple entrances from the powers of Set, and the protective human-headed sphinxes were developed from earlier carvings of lions. Also the twin-headed lion god Aker was a guardian of the entrance and exit of the underworld. It was his duty to ensure the safety of the sun god through his nightly passage.

Ram

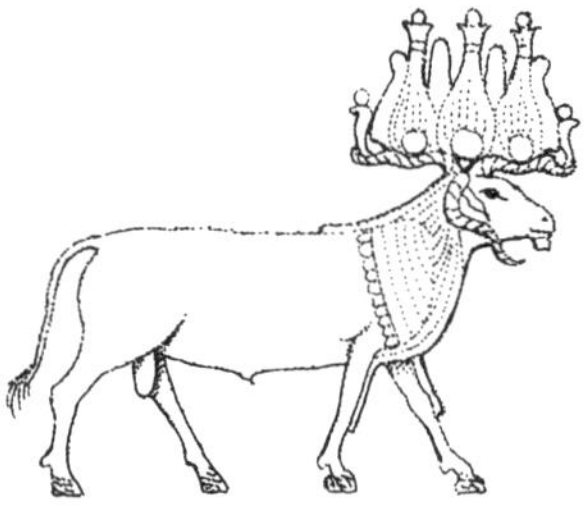

Various fertility gods appeared in the form of rams or had rams as their symbolic animal. The Ba of Osiris was believed to exist within the body of the sacred ram named Banaded, also known as the ram of Mendes. Later it was replaced by a goat which is referred to by the Greek Herodotus. When this animal died there was a great mourning, but likewise extensive celebrations followed the priest's discovery of the new Banaded.

Sacred rams were also worshipped at Elephantine and Esna as the god Khnum, and Amun was worshipped in the form of a ram as well.

Scorpion

The scorpion was the sacred creature of the goddess Selket, a minor goddess representing the heat of the sun, and she can often be seen wearing a scorpion upon her head as she keeps watch over the dead body of Osiris. In the story of Isis, seven scorpions protected her and Horus while they hid in the Delta. The scorpion was also worn as an amulet against evil.

Serpent

The serpent is another of the animals both revered and reviled by the ancient Egyptians. The gigantic serpent demon Apophis was the greatest enemy of the gods. It attacked the solar barque of Ra each morning and evening as it sailed across the threshold that separated darkness from light. Each day, however, the serpent was defeated by the crew of the barque and the skies became drenched red with his blood.

The serpent was also a symbol of Wadjet, the goddess of Lower Egypt, who sat upon the brow of both kings and gods protecting them from evil.

Other serpents were demons and helpers of Set. In wall paintings and elsewhere they are shown with legs or sometimes wings.

Vulture

The vulture was sacred to the goddess Mut and was venerated at her cult centre at Thebes. Seen spreading her wings protectively around her young whilst she fed them, the vulture was viewed as a symbol of motherhood by the Egyptians and so linked with Isis and Nephthys.

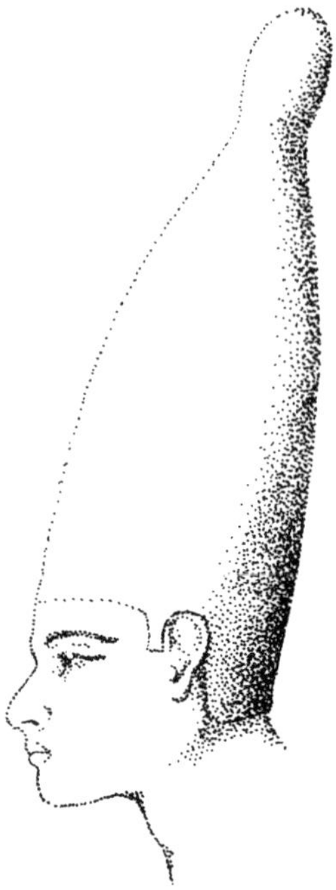

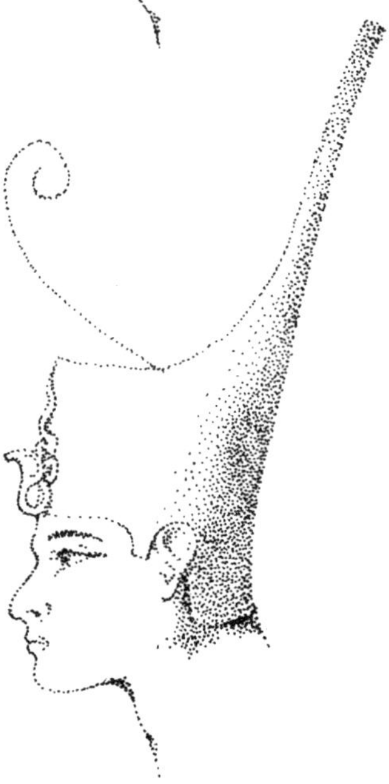

Crowns

The crown symbolized the power of the wearer, whether he be man or god, for such was the complex relationship between men and gods that titles and even family relationships became blurred. The god Osiris was believed to have once been an earthly king, for example, and each pharaoh was seen as a physical manifestation of Horus, becoming Osiris following his death. So it is common to see the various crowns of Egypt worn by both mortals and immortals.

Hedjet

The crown of Upper Egypt was the white mitre or conical hat known as the Hedjet. It was probably made of starched linen and resembled the bishop piece in the game of chess in shape. It was the symbol of Nekhebet, the goddess of southern Egypt.

Deshret

The crown of Lower Egypt was the red crown of the goddess Wadjet. It was flat topped with an extension at the rear reaching down the neck and also projecting above the wearer. The Deshret may originally have been made of reeds woven together as a basket, for a single reed curves out from the front on some representations.

Pschet

When the two kingdoms of Egypt became united both these crowns were combined and worn together as the Pschet. This double crown would have been heavy and clumsy to wear, and as such would only have been worn on special religious or state occasions. Kings are more often shown wearing a simple wig cover known as a 'nemes'. The nemes could be made of plain linen but it is usually shown striped and is at times further decorated with extensions which lie over the shoulders.

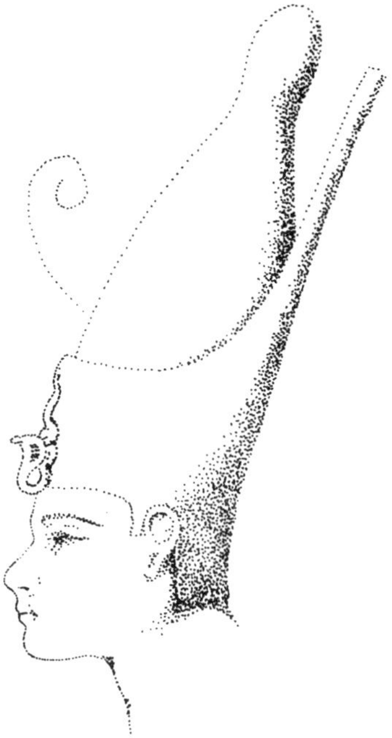

Khepresh or Blue Crown

The Khepresh is shown in sculpture from the Seventeenth Dynasty. Whilst it is called the war crown it was also worn on non-military state occasions and in private. The blue colouring of the wall paintings is symbolic, representing an outer skin of either electrum or bronze disks stitched or riveted onto a hardened leather base. The crown was usually finished off with two black streamers hanging down the back, and it may be possible that it was held in position by tying these together about the head.

Any of these crowns could be worn with the serpents head of Wadjet and the vulture of Nekhebet, the symbolic goddesses of the two Egypts. These were worn either individually with their respective crowns, or side by side with the united and blue crowns. These emblems, known as 'the two ladies', were believed to protect the wearer from harm, the serpent especially.

The Ka and the Ba

The ideas relating to the Ka are central to Egyptian religious belief. The Ka of a man was created at the moment of conception by the god Khnum on his potter's wheel, and lived in the body throughout his life. It was the etheric double of the body and could at times leave the body behind to travel alone, either in dreams or in what we would call astral projection.

When the body died the Ka divided into two parts, namely the Ba, which was the soul, and the Akh or the spirit. The Ba lived in the tomb within the body, however it was free to come and go as it pleased, moving around the tomb as it wished. For its comfort it was provided with all the necessities of the living—furniture, weapons, cosmetics, etc.

The Akh, as may be observed in tomb paintings, flew off to the otherworld in the form of a human-headed bird. These paintings also contain the writings known as *The Book of the Dead,* which provide instructions for the Akh on the correct ritual procedures for successful acceptance into the underworld.

So long as the Ba existed upon the earth the Akh was free to live for eternity in the otherworld, a joyous realm of the dead where other spirits walked with the gods in perpetual bliss and harmony. However should the body be destroyed, leaving the Ba homeless, then both it and the Akh would die the dreaded 'second death' that was so much feared by the Egyptians.

It was this overwhelming terror of the second death that led the Egyptians to spend so much time and effort on their funerary arrangements. Firstly the body underwent the elaborate preservatory process of mummification. Then the body was housed in a stone sarcophagus, within an almost impenetrable tomb, the pyramids being the ultimate examples. To deter the would-be tomb robber, the tomb and its contents was also protected by supernatural means using ritual magic and powerful curses. Finally, should the tomb be entered and the body destroyed, the Ba was provided with a statue of the deceased as an alternative home. This preoccupation with the mechanics of the afterlife permeated the whole of the Egyptian civilization. All that could be done to safeguard the Ba was done in the pursuit of eternal life.

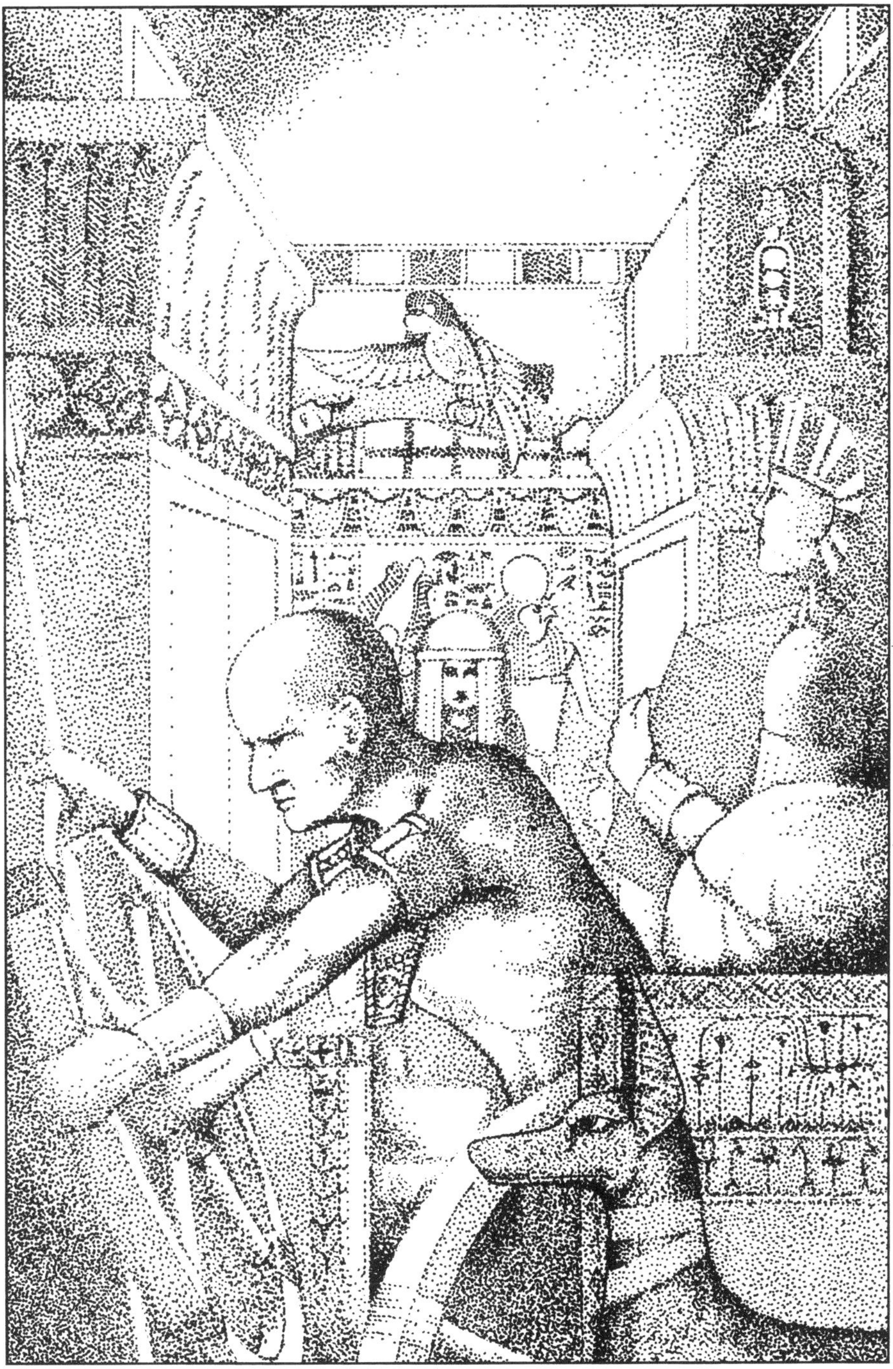

Sothis

Sothis was the Egyptian name for the star Sirius. To the Ancient Egyptians Sirius and the sun were the two most important heavenly bodies. Together they marked the start of the year and the annual inundation of the Nile. (Plutarch called the Nile by the name Sirius.) This occurred when the star was seen on the horizon just prior to the rising of the sun in the east. It was also close to the time when the sun moved into the constellation of Leo. Many centuries of observing this event enabled the architect Imhotep in 2686 BCE to plan the step pyramid at Saqqara with its entrance orientated towards this point. The Egyptians believed that it was the combined strength of the two heavenly bodies which caused the exceptionally hot weather that followed (now known as the Dog Days after the Dog Star, Sirius).

The Egyptians credited Thoth, the god of time, with the invention of the calendar. The year was made up of 3 seasons of 4 months. Each season was named after the main activity of that part of the year: the Flood, Planting and Harvest. Each month was made up of 3 weeks of 10 days each. A further 5 days (and 6 in every fourth year) completed the 365¼ day year. (The days themselves were divided into 10 hours of 100 minutes each, divided again into 100 seconds. This gave 100,000 seconds from midday to midday.) The additional 5 days were the birthdays of Osiris, Isis, Set, Nephytys and Horus. The owner of the extra leap year day is unknown but it has been suggested that it was ascribed to Thoth, as the month which followed, the first month of the year, was the month of Thoth.

The first day of the year was also the birthday of Hathor (whose temple at Dendera was aligned on the star Sirius), and was marked by great celebrations. Feasts were also held on this day to celebrate mankind's escape from the wrath of Sekhmet. In the pyramid texts both Hathor and Sekhmet are linked with the star Sept, which was another name for Sirius.

As the New Year's Day brought the life-giving floods it symbolized the rebirth of the land and was considered to be most auspicious. The official crowning of kings was performed upon this day.

Isis was the main deity associated with Sirius, and she was known as Sothis and also 'the lady of the star'. Osiris however was represented by the constellation of Orion, but this was due to a later misunderstanding. Sirius lies in the constellation known as Cannis Major, the great dog, and Osiris, like Anubis, his son and assistant in the underworld, was represented by the image of a dog.

Sirius is not a single, but a binary star, having a small dark partner known as Sirius B. Although known to the ancients, Sirius B was for a long time forgotten until its rediscovery in the last century. (The Dogon tribe of Mali, reputedly descended from predynastic Egyptians, have preserved traditions relating to the two stars, and tell of visitors arriving from Sirius in the distant past.) It is clear that Osiris was originally associated with Sirius B, the invisible companion of Sirius A. One of his titles was 'lord of perfect black' and he was a black god. This explains the importance of the Egyptian new year, for it was then that Isis and her husband, newly restored to eternal life by her skill and the aid of Thoth, appeared in the sky to herald the birth of their son Horus, the god of the sun, and proclaim the coming of the life-giving waters of the Nile to regenerate the earth.

The Pyramids

By the Fourth Dynasty (2600 BCE) the Egyptians had perfected the art of constructing pyramids. It was during this Dynasty that the great pyramids of Gizeh were built.

The form of the pyramid can be traced back to the flat-topped mastaba tombs of the early period, which were developed via the step-sided pyramid to the classic design. The choice of materials also developed: firstly unbaked bricks were used, then baked brick and finally skilfully cut and dressed stone.

Predynastic burials consisted of a pit, either rectangular or oval, dug into the ground, in which the body was placed in a crouched position and covered over with a mound of sand, the whole forming a structure not unlike the round-barrows of Europe. These graves contained not only bodies but personal possessions and vessels of food and drink, strongly suggesting a belief in the afterlife even at this early date.

Within the early dynastic period the form of the burial changed. Sand was an unreliable covering for the body, liable to be blown away by the wind at any time. So for the higher ranks in society it became common practice to construct a more permanent covering. This was in the form

of a platform of mud brick. This type of tomb is known as a mastaba, from the Arabic word for a low bench, which it resembled.

The mastaba tomb developed through the First Dynasty, being extended as time went on to provide secondary chambers. A brick superstructure above ground level was also divided into chambers. The exterior of these tombs was designed to resemble as closely as possible the houses of the time. Surrounding the main tomb would be rows of smaller tombs housing the deceased's servants, who were believed to attend his needs in the afterlife as they had done when he was alive.

At the beginning of the Third Dynasty King Djosr's prime minister was the great architect and scholar Imhotep. He designed and constructed the first step pyramid, originally only 8 metres high. After a series of extensions it eventually reached the height of 63 metres.

Later pyramids such as those at Meydum, built during the Fourth Dynasty, were originally constructed in steps, but then an outer course of polished limestone was added. Sneferu, also in the Fourth Dynasty, built a unique pyramid at Dahshur. This pyramid rises from the ground at a steep angle, then just below half its height it changes to a shallower angle for the rest of the way. A second pyramid built by Sneferu at Dashur was constructed from the outset as a true pyramid. The only difference between this and later constructions lay in the angle of the sides—where this pyramid had sides angled at 43° 36″ from the base, the later examples have angles of 52°.

By the Fourth Dynasty the layout of the pyramid was firmly established and quite rigid, although it became more relaxed during the Middle Kingdom. The entrance faced north towards the pole stars. At that time the star closest to the pole was not Polaris but Thuban in the constellation Dracco, the great cosmic serpent, the symbolic foe of the sun gods. The Egyptians called the pole stars the imperishable ones as they never set, and it was amongst these stars that the Akh or spirit was believed to reside after death.

The central chamber of the tomb in which the body of the deceased lay faced to the west towards the kingdom of the dead, whilst on the east lay the mortuary temple facing the rising sun.

The symbolism of the pyramid had two main elements. Firstly it represented the primal hill upon which Ra climbed out from the waters of Nun. Secondly it represented the rays of the sun falling upon the earth, providing sustenance for the Ba of the king within.

The finest achievements of pyramid building are those at Gizeh, which are also of this period. However with the rise of the Fifth Dynasty the great age of pyramid building was over. Other pyramids were built in later times but never again did the builders reach the excellence of the masons of the Fourth Dynasty.

Mummification

The origin of mummification is mythically attributed to both Isis and Anubis, with the body of the dead Osiris being the first to receive their embalming skills.

Historically the process had been perfected by the Fourth Dynasty. In all it took about 70 days from start to finish and comprised seven main stages.

1. Firstly the body was laid out upon the embalmer's table within a tent known as the 'place of purification'. A hooked implement was inserted into the cranial cavity via the nose, to cut up and remove the brain, an organ likely to putrefy rapidly.
2. An opening was made in the left-hand side of the lower abdomen through which the intestines, stomach, liver and lungs were removed. These were cleaned, dried and then after being individually wrapped in linen, deposited in four vessels known as canopic jars. The heart was not removed, for being muscle it was less prone to decay than the other internal organs. Also the heart was considered to be the seat of the intelligence and it was probably considered essential to leave it within the body.

3. The empty space within the body was filled with temporary packing to preserve its shape. This packing included natron (a compound of sodium carbonate and sodium bicarbonate), resin and other materials to promote dehydration.
4. The body was then left for a period of about 40 days to dry out fully. During this time it was covered with natron powder.
5. Afterwards the body was washed and the temporary stuffing removed and replaced with more permanent substances, including resin, sawdust, earth and in some cases even onions. The space left by the removal of the brain was filled with resin-soaked bandages.
6. Oils and ointments were used to anoint the body, and an eye of Horus amulet was placed over the abdominal incision.
7. The openings of the head were closed with either wax or cloth soaked in resin and the body was covered in liquid resin which, when hardened, would prevent the re-entry of moisture. It was then bound up in many layers of long bandages. Inserted into these wrappings were amulets, the quantity and quality of which depended upon the wealth and importance of the deceased.

It appears that the Egyptians went to considerable lengths to ensure that the finished mummy resembled the physical body of the deceased. Examples have been found where missing parts such as lost limbs have been made up from wood and cloth. In another mummy, that of Ramesses II, the nose was packed with small pearls to retain its shape.

Canopic Jars

The four containers into which the dried organs of the body were held are today known as canopic jars. Each jar bore the head of one of the four sons of Horus. These were Imset, Qebehsenuf, Duamuttef and Hapi, who received the liver, intestines, stomach and lungs respectively.

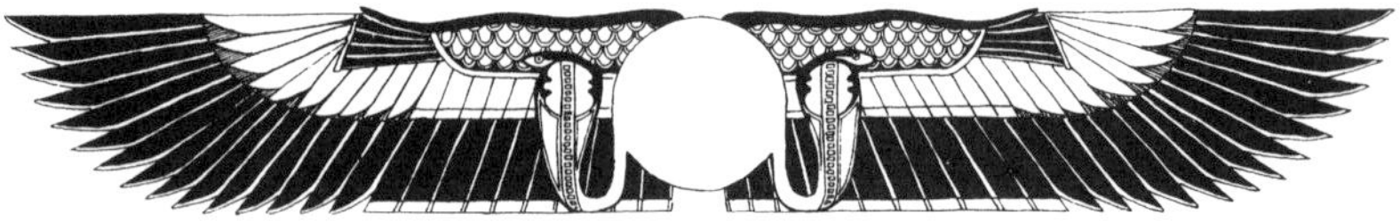

Symbols

Aegis

A small decorative shield in the form of a golden collar and often decorated with twin falcon or uraeus heads, the aegis was a symbol of protection.

Ankh

The ankh is oldest amuletic device of Egypt. The hieroglyphic sign of the ankh means 'life', 'living' and 'everlasting life'. It refers not only to the earthly world but also, and perhaps more importantly, to the afterlife, the second life, that of the spirit.

The symbol of the ankh combines the generative principles of man and woman in a single design. The loop represents the feminine reproductive organs while the remainder that of the male.

Another interpretation is that of a dam thrown across the Nile, which forms a lake of life-giving waters. The upright is the Nile, the cross bar the dam and the loop the lake.

Crook

The right to carry the crook was not restricted to gods and kings of Egypt but was also conferred upon high officials. Originally a shepherd's staff, it developed into the shorter sceptre carried over the shoulder by many Egyptian figures in both painting and sculpture. In hieroglyphics it signified the phrase 'to rule'.

Djed

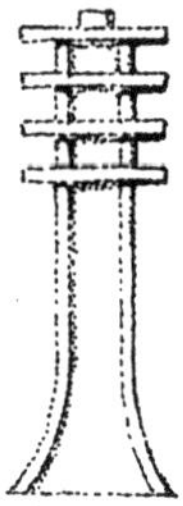

The djed was a symbol of the god Osiris and represented his backbone. As a hieroglyph it signified stability. A large-scale djed pillar was ceremoniously erected by each new king to magically confer stability upon his reign. This act also represented Osiris's resurrection in the new ruler and his consequent triumph over Set. Because of the djed's strong links with Osiris and the rites of the dead it became one of the most popular of funerary amulets.

Flail

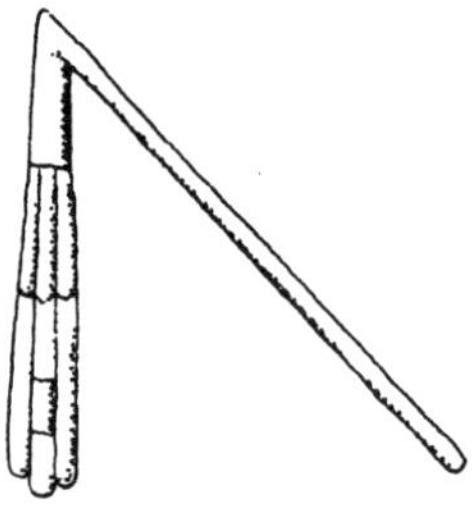

The flail consisted of a rod surmounted by three strings of beads and its origin has been attributed to both a fly whisk and a shepherd's whip. It was carried by the gods Osiris and Min, and also by the kings as a symbol of authority.

Lotus

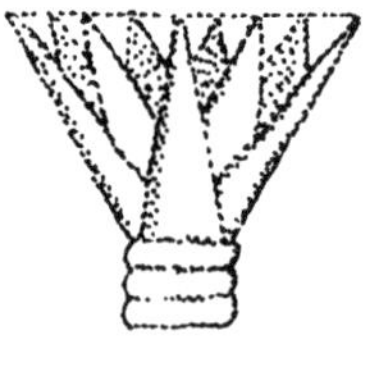

The lotus or water-lily was sacred to the solar gods, for at dawn the plant would mysteriously orientate itself towards the east as if honouring the rising sun. It was the heraldic plant of southern Egypt and appears often as a decorative feature in both art and architecture. In one wall painting guests arriving at a banquet are each presented with a lotus flower, which they wear in their headbands.

Mace

The mace, a stylized form of an ancient weapon, was a symbolic representation of the fiery eye of Horus. Many times in Egyptian art kings armed with a mace are shown defeating their enemies just as the eye of Horus was reputed to do. The mace was also believed to house the supernatural power of the king.

Nekhebet

Nekhebet was the national goddess of Upper Egypt, and the small vulture's head also called Nekhebet was worn beside the uraeus on the royal crown, symbolizing the joining of the two lands.

Papyrus

The papyrus plant represented the universe that came from the chaos of Nun. As the heraldic plant of Lower Egypt it is shown growing from the primeval mound. The papyrus wand was associated with Hathor and Bast, and both may be seen carrying it in wall paintings. A bunch of papyrus represented triumph and joy.

The Ring

Representing eternity, the ring was worn to provide protection against illness—it was an amulet for good health. It also represented the great year and the divine court of Osiris.

Sa

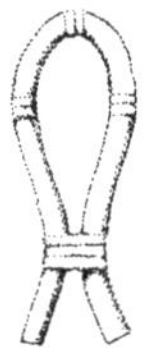

The Sa was an amulet ensuring protection, especially at the time of childbirth.

Scarab

The scarab beetle was sacred to the sun gods and as such a scarab amulet provided the wearer with the protection of the solar deities. Many small examples have been found with magical inscriptions carved on their undersides. The scarab was also placed in the tombs of the deceased as a symbol of rebirth in the afterlife.

Sekhem

This was the staff of office, the wand of power, for the word sekhem means literally 'power'. It also symbolized the stars and is found in paintings with both Osiris and Anubis.

Sistrum

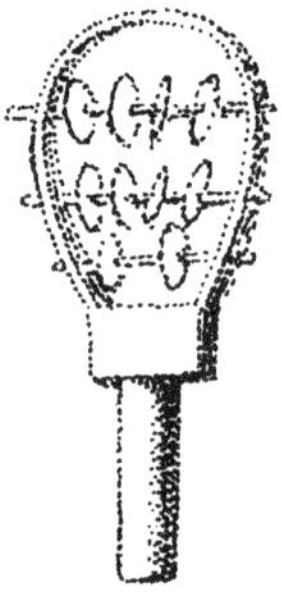

The sistrum is a musical instrument consisting of a hoop which holds three or four rods each bearing a number of loose metal discs. When shaken the discs rattle. The sistrum is associated with the goddesses Isis, Hathor and Bast, but as many of the examples we have are decorated with cats, it is reasonable to assume that its links with Bast are the oldest. The instrument was used to confer blessings and also its sound would ward off the powers of evil.

The Greek historian Plutarch writes that the loop of the sistrum represented the orbit of the moon around the earth, while the four rods symbolized the four elements.

Tet

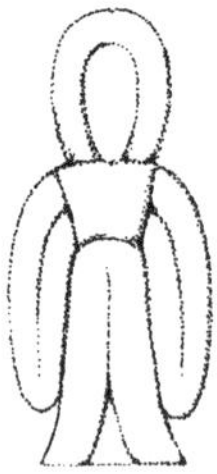

Also known as the blood of Isis, the origin of the tet is unknown but it resembles both ankh and the knot that tied the belts of gods. It is often shown with the djet, ıbolizing the union and combined ·ngth of Isis and Osiris.

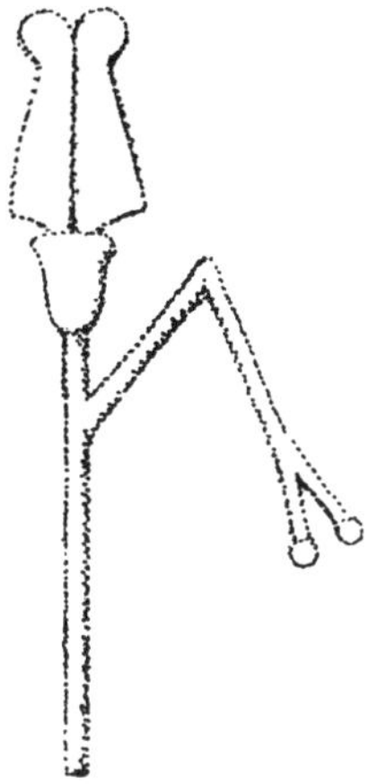

Uch

ated to the cult of Hathor, the uch wand ; a lotus crowned with two feathers. It resented the supporting pillar of ıven, and therefore strength.

Uraeus

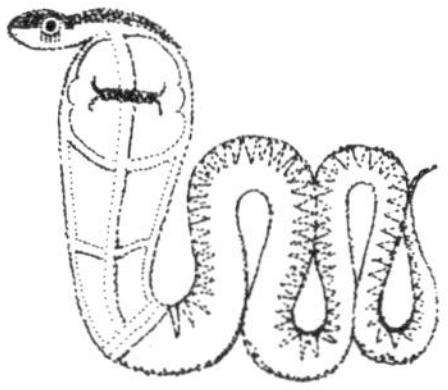

The uraeus, a rearing cobra with inflated hood worn upon the brow of the pharaoh, was the symbol of legitimate kingship. It represented the goddess Wadjet, the patron goddess of Lower Egypt. Geb gave the uraeus to the king as a symbol of his position and it was also worn by the gods Ra and Horus. In legend it had the power to spit fire in the defence of its wearer.

Waas Sceptre

The waas sceptre was a staff with a forked tail and the head of an animal, variously described as a fox, dog and even a phoenix. It was carried by both gods and kings as a symbol of good health, happiness and prosperity.

Wadjet Eye, Udjet Eye

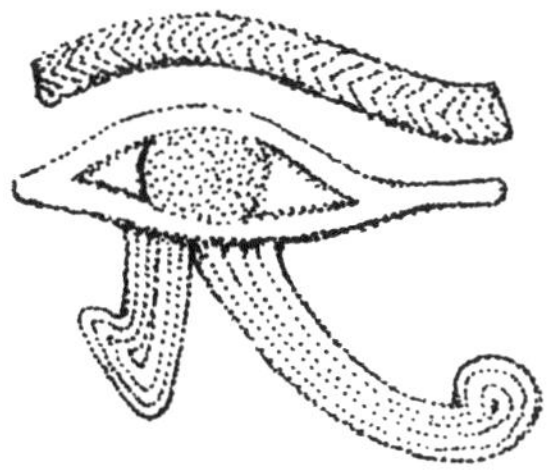

The eye of the moon which Set stole from Horus and which was later restored to him by Thoth, the wadjet eye was a popular amulet and would be worn to protect against evil. It symbolized the power of light embodied in the solar god Horus. It was also painted in pairs on coffins and sarcophagi to protect the enclosed body.

Index